Death, Burial, and Afterlife in the Biblical World

Death, Burial, and Afterlife in the Biblical World

How the Israelites and Their Neighbors Treated the Dead

by Rachel S. Hallote

Ivan R. Dee
CHICAGO 2001

 For information, address: Ivan R. Dee, Publisher, 1332 North Halsted Street, Chicago 60622. Manufactured in the United States of America and printed on acid-free paper.

Library of Congress Cataloging-in-Publication Data:
Hallote, Rachel S., 1965–
Death, burial, and afterlife in the biblical world : how the Israelites and their neighbors treated the dead / by Rachel S. Hallote.
p. cm.
Includes bibliographical references and index.
ISBN 1-56663-401-6 (alk. paper)
1. Death—Biblical teaching. 2. Burial—Palestine—History—To 1500. 3. Future life—Biblical teaching. 4. Palestine—Antiquities. 5. Dead—Religious aspects. 6. Death—Religious aspects—Judaism. I. Title.

BS1199.D34 H35 2001
296.4'45'0933—dc21

2001047148

Contents

	Preface	**5**
	Acknowledgments	**9**
	Introduction	**11**
1.	Death in the Biblical World	**27**
2.	The Cult of the Dead in Ancient Israel	**54**
3.	A History of Death in the Land of the Bible	**69**
4.	The Death Customs and Beliefs of Israel's Neighbors	**102**
5.	The Biblical Origins of Hell and the Devil	**123**
6.	Resurrection and Lack of Death in the Bible	**136**
7.	Death in Rabbinic Judaism	**150**
8.	Jewish Death in the Modern World	**169**
9.	A History of Mortuary Theory	**180**
10.	The Politics of Death in Israel	**194**
	Afterword	**208**
	Appendix	**210**
	Notes	**213**
	Bibliography	**223**
	Index	**228**

Preface

It was only my second season working on an archaeological dig in Israel when I came upon my first human burial. It was not a particularly exciting one, just a skeleton of a poor soul who had had the misfortune to be buried in what became an archaeological site. I spent the rest of that season and part of the next one learning how carefully to excavate human remains without breaking the large bones or losing the small ones, and learning how to tell what position the body was in so that I would not dig through part of it by accident.

I also learned how to cover my tracks and pretend I was not digging up a grave at all, so that the religious branch of the Israeli government would not shut down the excavation site because of the find.

The politics did not put me off. Remains of ancient burials are one of the most fascinating and informative sources for learning about the world of the Bible, and I was not deterred by the fact that excavating them is all but illegal in Israel. Instead I found myself several years later researching exactly what burials can tell us about the beliefs and cultures of the people of the Bible.

Figuring out some of the answers is rather tricky because the Bible does a good job of disguising how the ancient Israelites perceived death. What they really believed about death and afterlife was different from what they were supposed to believe, and the editors of the Bible were afraid that the truth would threaten the very foundations of the young, monotheistic religion.

What was it about the dead that was threatening to biblical religion? Most ancient Israelites worshipped their dead family members by feeding them and by praying to them. Why was this a problem? Because by worshipping their dead relatives they were breaking the first two of the Ten Commandments, which state that one may worship Yahweh, the one God, and no one else.

And what is it about digging up the dead that is currently threatening to the religious branch of the modern Israeli government? Any damage done to a body, alive or dead, is a violation of religious law. There is a fascinating parallel to the ancient world here: both ancient and modern religious leaders in Israel believed (and believe) that any deviant treatment of the dead could damage the religion of the Bible. More precisely, in both ancient and modern times, religious leaders have tried to suppress any "contact" between the living and the dead in order to maintain the status quo of the religion.

From its earliest stories the Bible presents death in a no-nonsense manner and gives examples of death-related customs that show the reader how he himself should act. For instance, early in the book of Genesis, Abraham, the first of the biblical patriarchs, buys a cave called Machpelah as a burial plot for his wife. The cave is not intended for his wife's remains alone, though. It is meant for his entire family—sons, daughters, nieces and nephews, even grandchildren, who will die in the future.

Family burial caves like this one were very common in Abraham's time (approximately 2000 B.C.E.), and were just as common a full thousand years later. These caves stayed in use for generations—family members would unseal them at every subsequent death to add the new body. When a cave became too crowded, the bones were simply pushed to the sides to make more room.

These burial caves were not unique to ancient Israel. They were commonly used by the polytheistic Canaanites. Why does Abraham, known as the first monotheist, bury his wife in the style of the Canaanites? As we shall see, death practices are the best possible evidence that the ancient religions in the land of the Bible were not nearly as different from one another as the Bible makes them out to be.

Another burial practice, the burial of family members under the floor of one's home, began at least four thousand years ago and continued nonstop for three and a half millennia. In the world of the Bible it was the second most common burial tradition, right after burial caves. This practice speaks volumes about the ancient preoccupation with family and the importance of caring for relatives both before and after they die. It also highlights inescapable contrasts with the way our own society distances itself from dying, death, and corpses.

At first glance ours is a culture that is not afraid to confront death. Major American cities experience several murders a day, which are casually reported on the evening news. Violence and gore are staples of recent blockbuster movies, and vampires abound on television. Yet in contradiction to this we have a deep-seated fear of death and a reluctance to let go of life. Most people request that hospitals exercise "extraordinary measures" to resuscitate loved ones. Our vocabulary is filled with euphemisms such as "passed on" and "gone."

Both our fearless and our fearful perceptions of death stem directly from the Judeo-Christian roots of our secular culture, and those roots are planted firmly in the Bible. Taking this even further, our various identities are reflected in and even formed by death and afterlife beliefs. This was true for the biblical world, and it is true today.

Acknowledgments

This book would not have been possible without the encouragement and support of many people, all of whom deserve enormous thanks. My greatest debt is to my husband, Alexander Joffe, who not only stood by me during the writing process but also helped with the research for the last chapter. My parents, Cynthia Ozick and Bernard Hallote, provided inspiration from the beginning and support throughout. My children, Sam and Rose, served as perfect and constant distractions. Pamela Gottfried kept me grounded in Jewish tradition on a weekly basis.

This book had several geneses, beginning in my student days at the University of Chicago and ending with a course that I developed and taught at the Pennsylvania State University. The list of scholars that I encountered along the way, many of whom helped me refine and improve my thoughts on death, is too long to recite. Ultimately, however, the ideas and opinions presented here are my own, and no one else is responsible for my errors.

Finally, my thanks to my agent Keith Korman and especially my editor Hilary Schaefer at Ivan R. Dee.

All translations are from the New Oxford Annotated Bible with the Apocrypha, Revised Standard Version (New York:

Oxford University Press), edited by Herbert May and Bruce Metzger.

I would like to dedicate this book to the memory of Douglas Esse, my teacher and mentor.

Introduction

Burial customs almost never change. They remain the same over generations, centuries, sometimes even millennia. Almost nothing can shake them, not wars, defeats, relocations, or cultural mixings.

Jewish burial customs have remained identical since the beginnings of the religion. In some ways they still reflect burial customs of the biblical world. The only significant changes that have occurred are in attitudes toward death rather than treatments after death, and these attitudes have shifted largely in the last 150 years as technological advances in embalming and then health care reached the masses, and as Jewish identities in the modern world evolved.

Why are burial customs so slow to change? What is it about death that makes experimentation an impossibility? Is it fear, and if so, fear of what? Is it respect, and if so, why is it so strong?

The fact is that the remarkable death practices of the biblical world—and those of early Judaism—reflect a cult so strong and so pervasive that even sworn enemies were united by it. Practicing this so-called Cult of the Dead gave people a way to preserve the memories of their immediate family members as well as their more distant ancestors long after they had died. Death practices also gave them a way to display their communal identities and ensure their own survival into the future.

But it was more than just preservation and survival. The Cult of the Dead kept dead ancestors active in current family life, giving them a sort of immortality. No one ever disappeared from the community—their roles just shifted slightly after they died.

The pull of immortality was strong, but the fear of revenge for not keeping up an ancestor's cult was probably stronger. The dead were part of the family, all right, and they were certainly venerated, but they were not trusted. They held the powers of giving sickness and health, and even the powers of life and death. With these powers they made frightening opponents, and no one wanted to test their goodwill.

These beliefs, or vestiges thereof, survived wars, conquests, exiles, and returns. They even survived interactions with other cultures. While encounters with other cultures added new beliefs to the postbiblical repertoire, no one ever abandoned the old ones, not even to this day. This makes biblical death practices truly remarkable.

The burial practices of the biblical world need to be discussed within a historical frame of reference. How far can the Bible be trusted on death-related issues? To determine whether the Bible presents the history of Israel accurately, we must first define what we mean by history. History is defined by writing; we learn about a historical period from contemporary written documents. Prehistory antedates writing; we learn about it chiefly from archaeological sources.

With writing as the defining item, the difference between history and prehistory should be clear-cut, and it is for many ancient cultures. Unfortunately the issue is more slippery for ancient Israel, because in Israel writing came extremely late.

Geographically, ancient Israel was sandwiched between two great powers, Egypt and Mesopotamia. In both these places writing began at approximately 3200 B.C.E. From that point forward, historians have access to countless lists, histories, biographies, and short inscriptions as well as many other texts.

By contrast, only a negligible number of biblical period inscriptions, and no long documents, have been found in Israel. Even the period of the Israelite monarchies (12th–6th C B.C.E.) has produced only a few short inscriptions, as no archive of any sort has been found in the country.

The Bible recorded many stories about the intimate (though not always desirable) relationships between Israel and its neighbors, and Egyptian and Mesopotamian texts also describe close economic and political relations.[1] Why would a society that has significant interactions with literate societies not have a writing system of its own?

It is possible that the royal archives of ancient Israel have simply not yet been found, that archaeologists will come across a trove of tablets at any time. Another possibility is that in ancient Israel, people wrote only on organic, perishable media, such as papyrus, or even paper. While papyrus famously survived in the extremely dry tombs of Egypt, it would not survive in the slightly wetter climate of Israel—nor would other organic materials.

Though plausible, neither of these explanations is particularly likely. More likely is that the ancient Israelites and the Canaanites before them were not record keepers, at least not for internal state business.[2] There is, however, good evidence for international correspondence—documents written by the Canaanites of the Late Bronze Age in Mesopotamian cuneiform, the lingua franca of the day, on Mesopotamian-style clay tablets.

These documents were found in Egypt, part of a much larger archive from the city of Amarna. The Amarna archive included letters from Canaanite princes, Mesopotamian kings, Nubian princes, and others. The archive proves that the Canaanites were literate, and it is likely that the Israelites who conquered them were also literate, at least once they settled in the land.

In the absence of written records, a history of early Israel must be pieced together by drawing on information gleaned from archaeology, written records from Egypt and Mesopotamia, and the Bible itself. The Bible must be used with caution as it was not intended as history but as a religious and political document. The difficulties in separating mythology from history, and in separating a historic kernel of a story from its religious and political intentions and accoutrements, are issues that bear directly on the study of the mortuary practices of the Israelites.

Did the stories of Adam and Eve in the Garden of Eden really happen? Was there in fact a man named Noah, and did he really build an ark that housed animals of every species during a catastrophic flood that lasted more than a month? Was there really a man named Abraham who journeyed from Ur in Mesopotamia to ancient Canaan because he had a monotheistic revelation?

Biblical stories are clearly imbued with religious ideas and ideals that are still integral to the three major world religions. Among biblical scholars, the minimalist school dismisses most of these stories as fiction, and the maximalist school accepts them intact. Even the minimalists agree that these stories reflect cultural aspects of some distant or not-so-distant past.[3]

Some of the most perplexing as well as the most important references to death, burial, and afterlife come from the earliest stories in the Bible. One of these concerns the death of Enoch, a man who lived in the murky mytho-history between Adam and Eve and Noah. Another of these concerns Abraham himself, who buried his wife in a Canaanite cave.

Until we know what an Israelite is, we will not be able to recognize an Israelite burial, and certainly will not be able to determine what the Israelites thought about death.

It is commonly believed that the Israelites emerged as a people at around 1200 B.C.E. According to the Bible, they came from Egypt via the Sinai desert, then attacked, conquered, and displaced the Canaanites who already lived in the land.

The Bible discusses the Canaanites as early as the Abraham narratives. Abraham, a somewhat renegade monotheist who migrated from Mesopotamia to Canaan, found the land already populated—"At that time, the Canaanites were in the land" (Gen. 12.6). He interacts with the Canaanites, pitching his tent near the Canaanite cities of Bethel and Ai (Gen. 12.8), and later moves to Hebron (Gen. 14.18).

The Bible is the best source for the subdivisions of the Canaanites. They are mentioned many times in the books of the Prophets as well as early on in Genesis. These biblical references are not only an acknowledgment that the Canaanites predated the Israelites in Canaan, they also present the Canaanites as integral to the stories of the Israelite forefathers.

This early material aside, the Canaanites figure most prominently in the latter part of the Hebrew Bible, especially in the books of Joshua and Judges, and in Numbers 13, in which Moses sends spies into Canaan. Moses' spies come back with the following report about the Canaanites:

> We came to the land to which you sent us, a land flowing with milk and honey, and this is its fruit. Yet the people who dwell in the land are strong, and the cities are fortified and very large; and besides, we saw the descendants of Anak (giants) there. (Num. 13.27–28)

According to this quotation, not only are the Canaanites strong, not only do they build and maintain well-fortified cities, they are actually giants of superhuman size. This notion is repeated in more than one context. Clearly the Israelites take the Canaanite presence in the land very seriously.

Another way of confirming that the Canaanites were in the land of Canaan before the Israelites got there is by extra-biblical texts. Mesopotamian and Ugaritic texts of the second and first millennia use the term "Kinahhu" and Egyptian texts use "Kinahni." The term originally referred to the red dye that the people of the northern Levantine coast made from the shells of a mollusk, the murex, found there. The Greek term for the red-purple color was "phoinix," from which the term "Phoenician" derives. The Phoenicians were the northern Canaanites.[4]

In the period called the Iron Age I (1200–1000 B.C.E.) Israelite settlements are generally limited to the highlands—the mountains in the middle part of Israel. These settlements have a specific courtyarded house type known as the four-room house. A certain pottery type is also associated with Israelite settlements—a jar with an extra rim of clay around its neck, known as the collared-rim storage jar.

The presence of these three features—location, house type, and pottery type—generally denotes an Israelite settlement. Their absence denotes a Canaanite settlement. These are not hard-and-fast rules, as Canaanites occasionally built four-room houses or bought or made collared-rim storage jars, but they serve as a general cultural barometer.[5]

As the Iron Age progresses, these three cultural items that distinguished Israelites from Canaanites disappear. The Israelites conquer the land and move beyond the central hill country. The Canaanites imitate Israelite house styles. The Israelites imitate Canaanite pottery styles. By the end of the Iron Age one cannot tell a Canaanite from an Israelite settlement. The biblically based assumption is that most settlements were by then Israelite, that the Canaanite enemies had completely assimilated into Israelite culture and religion.

But even at the height of their differences, the pottery and other material objects that the Israelites used in their day-to-day lives were virtually the same as those the Canaanites used. By and large, the Israelites shared the material culture of the

Canaanites in spite of the adversarial relationship of the two peoples. Most interesting for us, their burial customs were always indistinguishable.

During the twentieth century three basic schools of thought developed about the arrival of the Israelites in Canaan. All three concern the "second" arrival—not that of Abraham, the progenitor of a small tribe of Hebrews, but that of the twelve tribes of Israel returning to Canaan after living in Egypt as slaves. This second arrival is documented mainly in the book of Joshua and the book of Judges.

The first of the three schools was proposed by the renowned biblical and archaeological scholar William Foxwell Albright. Albright's theories were based in the book of Joshua. After the death of Moses, Joshua led the Israelites into Canaan, attacking and violently conquering one Canaanite city after another. He began with Jericho and Ai in the hill country, then followed a northern trajectory through the rest of Canaan.

Albright held that these stories from the book of Joshua were historically viable, that this is how the Israelites traveled to Canaan. But archaeological evidence shows that neither Jericho nor Ai was significantly occupied in 1200 B.C.E., much less completely destroyed.

Albright defended his theories by playing with the time frame of the Exodus and by using the fact that other cities in the vicinity did experience major destructions at about this time, even if Jericho and Ai did not. Still, a Joshua-based history remains problematic.

The second theory was put forward by the German scholar

Albrecht Alt. Rather than following the account of Joshua, Alt looked to the book of Judges as a model. In Judges the Israelites settle the land of Canaan peacefully, establishing small Israelite outposts between the large Canaanite cities. There were conflicts only later, at the end of this period of peaceful infiltration, once the Canaanites finally perceived the Israelites as a threat.

Alt's theory is also not perfect. If there were no significant conflicts in the early part of this period, why does the archaeological record show that some cities were in fact destroyed?

A third approach deviates from both biblical accounts. It is a sociological one, first proposed by George Mendenhall and expanded by Norman Gottwald. It is colloquially known as the "peasant revolt" theory and was considered revolutionary because it postulates that neither the story in Joshua nor the one in Judges reflects the true emergence of Israel. Instead Mendenhall and Gottwald suggested that the Israelites began as a fringe group of Canaanites, poor and heavily taxed, who were eventually incited to rebel. They moved away from the coastal cities of the Canaanites into the central hill country where they remade themselves as Israelites. Once there they adopted the god Yahweh after an encounter or a merger with a Yahwist group from Edom. Eventually Yahweh supplanted the Canaanite gods.

If the Israelites really were Canaanites, it would explain why their material cultures and their burial practices were so similar. But what about the Exodus story of the slave rebellion from Egypt and Moses leading the people through the desert to Canaan?

There is no mention of any slave rebellion in Egyptian sources, and the single Egyptian mention of an ethnic group called Israel refers to a people already living in the open plains of Canaan. Nonetheless several maximalist scholars have attempted to reconcile a Canaanite origin for the Israelites with the Exodus story of the Bible, while minimalists are willing to dismiss the Exodus unilaterally.

The burial practices of the Israelites and the Canaanites must be looked at together, as one emerged from the other, and the other blended back into the first.

In approximately 920 B.C.E. King Solomon died. A civil war followed his death, and Israel, which had been one political entity until that point, split in two. From that point forward there was a northern kingdom, which retained the name Israel, and a southern one, which called itself Judah.[6]

Two countries now existed rather than just one. Each had its own king and its own political system. Each had its own prophets. Each even had its own sets of enemies. The only items they shared were their joint histories and their monotheistic religion, a belief that Yahweh was the only god.

The capital city of Judah was Jerusalem, a city that had been taken from the Canaanites by King David. Not only did Jerusalem contain the royal palace, but the Temple to Yahweh was there as well. This Temple was supposed to be the one and only Temple dedicated to Yahweh.

When the kingdom split in half, the Temple no longer belonged to all the Yahwists but only to those who lived in the southern kingdom of Judah. The northern Israelites, also Yahwists, built their own capital city, Samaria, but they lost the Temple.

These northern Israelites could not (and would not) cross a political border to worship in the capital city of the Judahites, yet they still wished to worship Yahweh. Their only recourse was to build shrines to Yahweh in several cities of their own country, notably but not exclusively in the city of Dan, at the northern tip of their territory, as far from Jerusalem as it was physically possible to go.

The existence of Yahweh worship outside of Jerusalem pitted the southern kingdom against the northern one. In the view of the southern Judahites, the northerners were sinning by sacrificing to Yahweh outside of Jerusalem. They were also sinning by interacting with certain groups of Canaanites among whom they lived.

Gradually the southern Judahites stopped considering the northern Israelites members of the same religion. By late antiquity, Judahites, or Jews as they came to be known, were a separate entity from "Samaritans," that is, the people of Samaria (Israel), whose religion survived on a small scale even after their kingdom was destroyed.[7]

The rest of the history can be told briefly and simply. The northern kingdom of Israel was destroyed in 722 B.C.E. by the Assyrians, a Mesopotamian people known for their ruthless disregard for life as well as for their empire building. Assyria had a policy for dealing with the citizens of conquered territories, and the fate of most of the so-called ten lost tribes of Israel was determined by that policy. The Assyrians deported all their war captives, scattering them in small groupings throughout their vast empire. This scattering effectively broke down national loyalties as well as clan allegiances. Within a few generations the deportees forgot their origins and assimilated into Assyrian society—and this is what happened to the majority of the Israelites.

The southern kingdom of Judah lasted 136 years longer than its northern neighbor. Judah was destroyed by the Babylonians in 586 B.C.E. The people of Judah were exiled as a single group to Babylon, though a contingent escaped to Egypt.

In Babylon the Judahites were known as "people from Judah," a term which came into many languages intact ("Jud" in German, "Judaism," "Jew," in English). In this book "Judahites" refer to the people before 586 B.C.E.; "Israelites" to the northern kingdom of Israel or the United Monarchy; and "Jews" to the period after 586 B.C.E.

The geographical and cultural circumstances of biblical peoples matter because the Bible itself was written by the religious and political establishment of the southern kingdom of Judah. While the Bible incorporates many stories of the northern kingdom of Israel, it is primarily a southern religious document. Practically that means that the text praises Judah and criticizes Israel, the Canaanites, the Philistines, and anyone else who did not share Judah's strict, Jerusalem-centered Yahwism. Biblical criticism of northern Israel often states that the Israelites were backsliding, worshipping like the Canaanites worshipped. One of the worst ways the Israelites backslid (according to the Judahites) was by taking part in Canaanite rituals associated with the Cult of the Dead. That is why the chronology and history of Israel and Judah is so important for talking about death, burial, and afterlife in the biblical world.

The Judahites themselves recognized similarities between

their own death practices, those of the northern Israelites, and those of their enemies. They despised those similarities but could do nothing to change them. The Cult of the Dead was so deeply entrenched in everyday practice, such an unchangeable facet of the popular religion, that in spite of prophetic whining it survived beyond the destruction of Judah itself.

Death, Burial, and Afterlife in the Biblical World

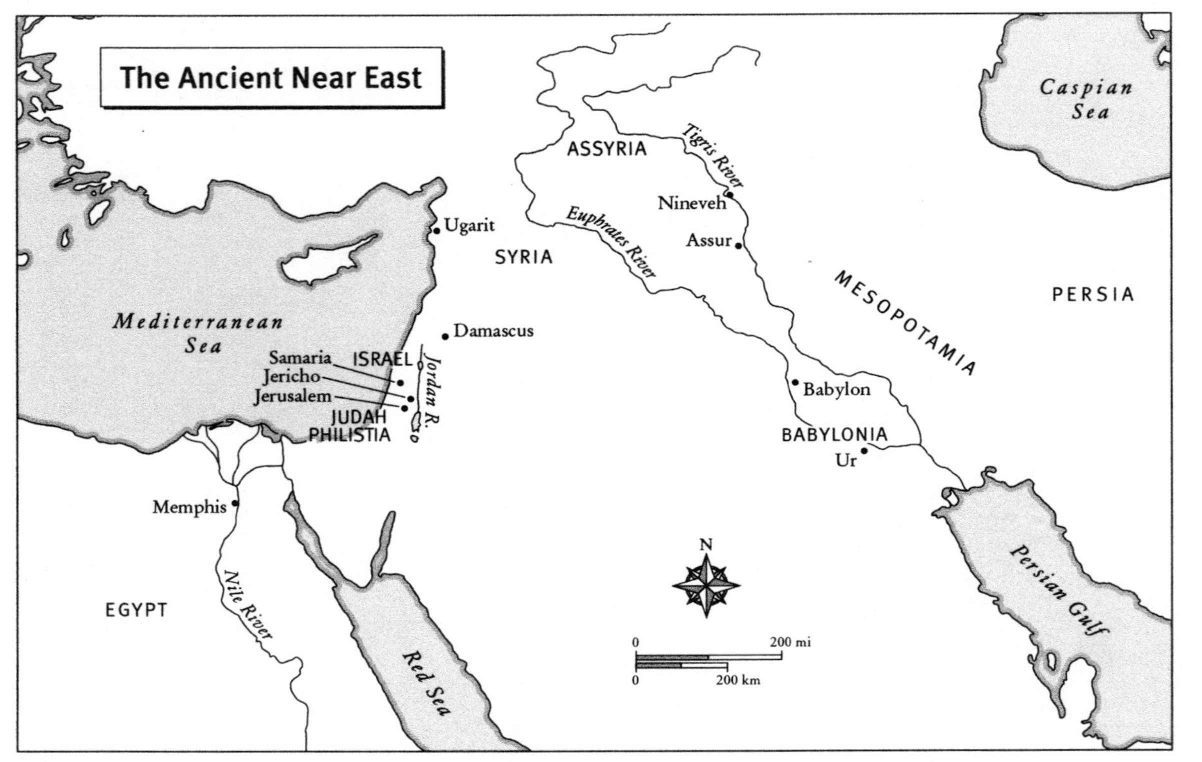

The Ancient Near East
Caspian Sea
PERSIA
ASSYRIA
Tigris River
Nineveh
Assur
Euphrates River
SYRIA
Ugarit
Damascus
MESOPOTAMIA
Babylon
BABYLONIA
Ur
Persian Gulf
Mediterranean Sea
Samaria
Jericho
Jerusalem
ISRAEL
JUDAH
PHILISTIA
Jordan R.
Memphis
EGYPT
Nile River
Red Sea
N
0
200 mi
0
200 km

1

Death in the Biblical World

Research into beliefs about death and afterlife in the biblical world goes back almost as far as biblical scholarship itself. One of the most important points about discussions of death in the biblical era is that there is no biblical "handbook" on death. Scholars need to cull references to death beliefs and customs from throughout the Bible. This means that diverse texts spanning the centuries are mixed together. It was not until much later, during the Rabbinic period, that religious leaders first tried to organize the material into some sort of manual.

The rabbinic sages were not completely successful in this endeavor. They could not put together a true manual from unrelated, sometimes contradictory, texts. Instead they merely searched the Bible for death references. Modern scholars have several advantages that the rabbinic sages lacked. These include a greater understanding of the time frames of the Bible, including the fact that its stories reflect different chronological periods. Modern scholars also have a better understanding of the intermingled political and social agendas of the Bible.

The two methodologies for learning about the death practices of the biblical world are archaeological research and biblical research. They must be used in tandem, as they serve as a system of checks and balances for each other. The information that follows comes from these two sources equally.

Euphemisms for the Dead

Today we use many euphemisms to describe the dead: a person has "passed away," "passed on," "gone to heaven," or "is no longer with us." Not all our euphemisms are pleasant. Some, such as "kicked the bucket" and "pushing up daisies," play into an urge to disguise death with humor.

The Bible also uses a variety of terms to describe the dead. Pleasant biblical euphemisms for the dead include "souls," "divine ones," "healers," "holy ones," "knowing ones," and "those who pass over." Less pleasant terms include "dead ones," "mutterers," "ghosts," and "corpses."

Most of these terms are found in a single book, the Book of Isaiah. Isaiah was a prophet who lived in Judah when Israel was destroyed by the Assyrians. His book is a collection of warnings to the Judahites—if they do not stop sinning, they will be destroyed just like their Israelite neighbors were destroyed. Isaiah wrote about death largely in the abstract, poetic language of prophecy, yet he does not shy away from the actuality of death.

Most of the terms Isaiah used for the dead were positive,

euphemistic ones. The dead were referred to with such praise because the Judahites (and the Israelites) believed that the dead still had a powerful role in the lives of the living. A dead person could take vengeance on someone who insulted him. The dead demanded praise because they inspired fear.

Another reason for praising the dead was that, if treated properly, they could be helpful. They could heal the sick if they chose, and in at least one biblical instance could even resurrect other dead persons.

The powers of the dead were both awe-inspiring and frightening. Fear of the dead and their powers, and the hope that dead ancestors would help rather than harm, went a long way toward solidifying burial practices and associated death rites.

The Continued Role of the Dead in Biblical Society: The Dead as Territorial Place Holders

Today we bury our dead and forget about them. At most we visit the gravesite at the anniversary of the death, placing flowers on it or, according to a Jewish custom, stones. We remember the dead and the role they played in our individual lives and in our communities, but we remember these roles as something of the past. When someone dies in modern society, his professional and personal standing die with him, and he is replaced in short order. His job is refilled, any volunteer community positions he held are refilled, and, after a period of mourning and adjustment, even his family evolves into a new configuration in which he is not involved.

This is not so in the biblical world. When someone died in

ancient Israel, his roles in the community and family certainly changed, but they did not disappear. Both the type and the place of burial reflect this.

One of the most intriguing pieces of evidence that archaeologists have for the continued role of the dead in the society is the location of the community's burials. Cemeteries were only one of three options for the placement of the dead in the biblical world. The dead were also buried under the floors and in the walls of individual houses or in the middle of open fields.

Of these three options, cemeteries are the most easily understandable since we still use these specialized areas today. A biblical-period cemetery was typically placed near the city but not within its walls. Sometimes a cemetery would be very close to the settlement, perhaps even on the slopes of the city's fortifications. Other times a cemetery would be as much as a kilometer away from the settlement with which it was associated.

A large cemetery from the several hundred years of the Iron Age might contain fifty or one hundred tombs, with perhaps twice that number of individuals interred. But the population of a typical urban unit of the Iron Age consisted of perhaps one hundred or two hundred individuals at any given time. Archaeologically speaking, a lot of dead are missing.

Although it does seem that they are missing, more accurately some dead have become invisible. The number of skeletons in a cemetery of a particular site represents only a fraction of the population.[1] Where are the other bodies? The answer is vital to mortuary archaeology. The other dead have disappeared—they are buried so carelessly that they did not survive the centuries.

For archaeologists who study burials, the criteria for deciding who gets buried, and where and how carefully people get buried, are the main windows into a group's culture.

Some of the criteria are obvious. Every complex society including biblical Israel has a social hierarchy. There are individuals of high rank and low rank; there are kings and there are peasants and slaves. Complex societies usually have additional differentiations as well, based on gender, age, health, even intelligence.

In ancient Israel we should and do see burials of rich as well as poor individuals. As expected, more time and attention went into the burial of the richer members of society than into the burials of their poorer neighbors. We also see differing treatments of adults and children.

The burials we see, be they rich or poor, do not represent the whole of society. Were the others not given burials at all? In the biblical world, everyone deserved a burial, even an enemy that had just been killed in battle. Not everyone is represented in the extant burials because most of society—specifically the lower classes—did not receive the type of burials that survive in the archaeological record.

Burials known from the biblical world range from rock-hewn tombs, to masonry-constructed tombs, to pits in the sand. Almost all of these leave a trace. The largest and most elaborate tombs survive well enough for archaeologists to find them intact thousands of years later. Even the least elaborate tombs that archaeologists find have some distinguishing feature, such as a selection of pottery vessels placed next to the body, or a brick platform on which the body rests.

But there are dozens if not hundreds of pits excavated around Israel that contain no bones at all but which are nonetheless correctly called tombs, based on their locations and on the type of items found in them.

If a skeleton eroded away completely due to poor conditions, and if no grave goods accompanied it, there will be no trace of that individual at all in the archaeological record. And many individuals were given very simple burials, interred in unlined, earthen pits. Sometimes the soil is so acidic that the bones of the skeleton have been completely eaten away. Sometimes the skeleton is displaced or destroyed by an earthquake (there is a fault line within Israel). In these situations, it is very easy for a plain burial, with no grave goods to make it recognizable as such, simply to disappear from the archaeological record.

This means that all the burials that archaeologists do find are of a pre-selected group of individuals. While there were certainly rank differentiations among them, they are all from the top strata of the society—individuals who warranted some sort of distinguishing burial treatment. The burial treatment may not have been fancy, but it was enough to make the burial recognizable to archaeologists, no matter what the condition of the bones themselves. The burials of the lowest strata of biblical society did not survive at all.

Status seems more or less simple to recognize in the archaeological record. A tomb with many offerings may denote a wealthy, upper-class individual, and a tomb with few offerings may denote someone less wealthy. Archaeologists have to be very careful making such claims. Some societies and religions, such as Judaism in the Talmudic and modern periods, prohibit fancy burial treatments no matter what the social and economic status of the deceased. Plain burials do not always mean a lack of wealth.

The converse is true as well. Members of some societies will put all the wealth they have into their burials, making it seem as if they were burying elites, when the truth is they were not.

In biblical Israel, status is pretty straightforward. There is no evidence of reverse elitism, either from the archaeological record or contemporary texts. As far as wealth goes, what you see is what you get.

Burial locations, by contrast, do not mirror economic or social status but instead reflect the role that the deceased play in the society after death.

Location 1: Burials in Open Fields

It is unclear how many burials were placed in open fields in the biblical period. Many of the older excavation reports and even some of the newer ones are not always specific about tomb locations. A full 50 percent of Middle Bronze Age tombs, for example, are not in large cemeteries or within settlements. The figure for the Iron Age is a less dramatic 20 percent.

Why were people burying their family members in the open, away from ancestral burial places and far from the houses where they lived? At first glance it might seem like a mark of disrespect, but it was just the opposite. These individuals were being trusted with an extremely important job—after they died, they became the guardians of the fallow fields.

In most agriculturally based societies, leaving some fields

fallow each year is normal procedure. This practice allows the land to rest, and the minerals that crops take from the soil are gradually replenished. Fallow farming (also known as crop rotation) was particularly vital in the ancient Middle East, where water was scarce. Numerous studies have looked at the destructive effect of salinization of the soil in Mesopotamia, a problem exacerbated by continual farming. The Bible itself mandates leaving all of Israel fallow every seventh season—the Sabbatical year (Lev. 25.1–7). An even more stringent Sabbatical was to take place every forty-ninth year (seven times seven) (Exod. 23.10–11, Lev. 21.1–7, Deut. 15.1–3, 9–10). This religiously sanctioned Sabbatical was observed strictly from the biblical through the Talmudic periods, and is even nominally observed in the modern state of Israel, albeit with significant loopholing. In practical terms, leaving a field fallow allows the soil to replenish the natural minerals needed to grow a better crop the following year.

When a crop is growing in a field it is clear to whom that field belongs, since the owner walks through it on a regular basis, threshing, planting, watering, and harvesting. But when a field lies fallow, especially a large field whose borders are far from the landowner's homestead, how can the landowner claim his field and keep his potentially dishonest neighbors from farming it? Such a field needs to be guarded, night and day, preferably by a very formidable guard whom no dishonest neighbor would dare test. A dead ancestor makes the perfect guard.

But not any dead ancestor. A woman or child, or anyone

else who lacked significant prestige in the society while alive, would not effectively scare away land robbers. But a community elder, or a clan leader, would make a perfect guard in the afterlife. Guarding the land was an important role for dead ancestors in ancient Israel, and this role explains why burials were sometimes placed away from cities.

Unfortunately excavators have not always properly recorded information regarding the age and gender of the buried. It does appear, however, that burials in open fields were usually adult males, confirming the use of the dead as land guards. The practice of placing graves in fields was still common in the Talmudic period. The agricultural tractate Pe'ah—part of the Mishnah, the first section of the Talmud—refers rather casually to graves in the middle of plowed fields. Tombs were still expected features in fields in this period, and according to the Mishnaic rule—the Oral Law taken from the first part of the Talmud—they could serve as a boundary to divide one field into two.

A single ancestor in a tomb could serve as a field guardian, but tombs with more than one individual were more common for these locations in the Iron Age. Shaft-and-chamber tombs (a type to be described in more detail below) often included multiple burials, most likely of family members. Entire families or members of extended clans could be placed in the fields as guardians.

Location 2: Tombs Under Houses

One of the most remarkable burial practices of the ancient Mediterranean world is the burial of the dead under floors of houses that were still being used. As with the case of burials out in the fields, this particular choice of location reflects the role of the deceased in life as well as in death. Children and adults and men and women could be buried within houses.

These tombs were almost certainly visible long after they were sealed. The spot would be subtly marked, often by the plaster of the floor, which would come up to the lip of the tomb but not hide it. These tombs also protruded several centimeters out of the floor, serving as constant reminders of those interred inside. When the living members of the household walked across a room, did their cooking, or went to bed, they would always be aware of the dead sleeping beneath their floors.

In the Bronze and Iron Ages, houses were intended to accommodate extended families rather than nuclear ones. Houses were structured around a courtyard, and various family members lived in each of the nonwork rooms surrounding that courtyard. Grandparents would still reside in the house where they were born, married sons would bring in their wives and move into the room that once belonged to their parents.

As families grew and shifted the space in the house was reallocated. Occasionally additions were made, but in many cases floor plans remained identical for a century at a time. The older generations especially would move from room to room each time there was a new marriage or new birth. When a member of the oldest generation died, he would simply be given another space within the house—this time beneath its floors. His final resting place kept him within the family unit in the most literal sense and allowed him to continue to participate in the life of the family and the household, even after death.

Tombs in houses were either plain pits dug into the dirt floor or more elaborately treated pits. Often they were either rounded or rectangular stone substructures, with stone shafts coming up to floor level. One or two individuals were placed in each.

The family members placed below the houses were in most cases both the young and the old, but not those in between. Those who needed caretaking were placed under the floors of the family home, not those who were thought to be strong enough to guard the land, for instance. The home was a space reserved for dead who had been the weaker members of the family when alive. This explains another phenomenon of biblical period burials, that of infant burials in storage jars.

The phenomenon of burying infants and young children who had died prematurely in storage jars under the floors of houses was a practice that began in prehistoric times but gained popularity in the Middle Bronze Age. In that period 17 percent of house sites have infant jar burials under their floors. By the beginning of the Israelite Iron Age the number has fallen to 14 percent.[2]

Infants in jars can also be found in cemeteries that are located very close to ancient settlements, but they are never found at any distance from the settlement. They are also never found alone, without an adult burial nearby. The reasons for this have to do with caring for infants even after death. This is why they were placed under floors and always close to an adult.[3]

High rates of infant mortality were common in the premodern world, and most societies responded to infant deaths in a manner different from their response to adult deaths. The Israelites and the Canaanites responded to infant deaths by putting them in storage jars. A likely explanation for doing this was that it seemed like the most appropriate approach. A storage jar is a small, enclosed space, in many ways reminiscent of the womb, which the infant had left only recently. Burying an infant in a womblike space returned it to the home it knew in life.

The idea of a tomb as a womb for infants is very much in line with the idea of a tomb as a house for adults.

A great deal of literature discusses tombs as houses for the dead in the ancient world. Some of the best-known studies are by Ian Hodder, who found that tombs in prehistoric Europe corresponded in shape, construction, orientation, position of entrance, and decoration to houses of the same period. Another region with striking and intentional similarities between tomb and house is ancient Egypt, where tombs were clearly built with rooms, corridors, false doors, and windows.

Because neither the tombs nor the houses of biblical-period Israel were particularly elaborate to begin with, fewer specifics are comparable. In spite of this, we still find convincing similarities between tomb and house.

With the exception of the simple pits, most burials in ancient Israel had some sort of architectural structure. Those below houses were often built of masonry and shaped into circles or rectangles. These architectural tombs also have masonry shafts as entrances.

The tomb-as-house parallels are as simple as they are clear. The main "living area" of the tomb is where the body or bodies are placed, and the entrance represents the doorway to a home. The mourners bring the deceased "home" to this familiarly shaped structure.

The parallelism is even clearer in another category of tombs—shaft-and-chamber tombs. Although they were man-made specifically for burial, researchers sometimes refer to these as "caves." In the Bronze Age they are irregular, roundish chambers cut into rock or sometimes into the hardened slopes of a city's ramparts. These are the tombs that make up cemeteries. In Genesis the "Cave of Machpelah," which Abraham buys as a burial place for his wife and where he himself is later buried, almost certainly refers to a man-made shaft-and-chamber complex rather than a natural cave. No single word in either English or Hebrew distinguishes between man-made and natural caves.

By the Israelite Iron Age, shaft-and-chamber tombs are extremely regular in shape. Researchers refer to these regular tombs as acrosolia. Acrosolia, as well as their earlier, rounder predecessors, generally consist of a shaft leading down to a central chamber. One to eight chambers open off of the central chamber. The bodies were laid in individual rooms.

In the Bronze Age versions of shaft-and-chamber tombs, each of these side chambers might contain a multiple burial, but by the Iron Age, when the chambers had become regular and rectangular, each has space only for a single individual. In spite of this, it is quite common to find a second skeleton crammed into a space obviously intended for a single one, and sometimes even the central "courtyard" space contains burials.

Sometimes these rectangular rooms had benches on which the bodies were laid, and sometimes the benches even had headrests carved out of stone.

It is easy to see the tomb-as-house parallels in the shaft-and-chamber tombs. Houses in antiquity were often centered on courtyards. Even the so-called "four-room" house style that is specifically associated with the Israelites is centered on a courtyard. In a house, the courtyard has several rooms opening from it, including living quarters, kitchen space, and other activity areas. These rooms can be reached only from the courtyard, not from outside the house.

The same is true of the tomb plans. In the case of the tombs, the rooms that open from the courtyard mimic the "living quarters" of the houses in that this is where the body will physically remain. Much as individuals spend significant portions of time in the activity rooms of a house, they will spend eternity in these rooms after they die. As in a house, the courtyard provides the only access to the individual rooms.

Just as people added to their houses—another room when a son married—tombs could grow as well. Even the most well-planned acrosolia would be cut one chamber at a time, as needed, rather than being dug out all at once.

These tombs almost certainly housed family groups. Just as tombs under houses were for family members, not strangers, tombs in cemeteries were also for family or kin groupings. Extended families shared a single subdivided house during life and then shared a single subdivided house during death.

Location 3: Cemeteries

Cities of the living are made up of many houses in a conglomerate. With a few notable exceptions such as Samaria and Beer Sheba, Israelite cities developed organically rather than being forced into orthogonal plans. Streets would meander, and people would add new houses against the backs of older ones as the needs of the households and of the community as a whole evolved.

Cemeteries of the biblical period grew in much the same way as cities did. When we talk about ancient Egypt, the close neighbor of Israel, we talk about "cities of the dead" because of their enormous size and the enormous amount of space they used. The same phrase can be used to describe some modern American cemeteries, where tightly packed tombstones sprawl along the urban countryside, dominating it completely either by choice or happenstance. While the cemeteries of ancient Israel are on a much smaller scale (everything about ancient Israel is on a small scale), they are also cities of the dead, cities of just the right size for the small cities of the living they serve.

Cemeteries in Israel sometimes consist only of a half-dozen shaft-and-chamber tombs but other times include hundreds of them, each housing multiple interments. Cemeteries are often near settlements but may also be at a small distance from them, and sometimes are placed near water, either a wadi or a spring. And like cities, cemeteries grew organically, according to need, rather than according to a planned arrangement.

The Bible uses a particular expression time and again when referring to deaths of important individuals. It is to "gather" or "collect" ("asaf" in Hebrew) a person to his ancestors. In the past, scholars of the Bible read this metaphorically, but taking the textual evidence together with archaeological evidence, we see that it is no mere metaphor. This is the Bible's way of describing family tombs and the Israelite custom of moving older interments to make room for newer ones.

The phrase is used in both early and late biblical narratives. Abraham, forefather of the Israelites,

> breathed his last and died in a good old age, an old man and full of years, and was gathered to his people. (Gen. 25.8)

The narrative goes on:

> Isaac and Ishmael his sons buried him in the cave of Machpelah, in the field of Ephron the son of Zohar the Hittite, east of Mamre, the field which Abraham purchased from the Hittites. There Abraham was buried with Sarah his wife. (Gen. 25.9–11)

The fact that Abraham is interred together with his wife demonstrates that the cave of Machpelah was a family tomb. In fact, Abraham intended it to be his family's tomb when he initially acquired it. This cave was almost certainly a shaft-and-chamber tomb of the sort described above, that is, intended for extended families.

The phrase occurs again when Moses' brother Aaron dies. "And Aaron shall be gathered to his people" (Num. 20.26). Another occurrence concerns the death of the entire generation of people that Joshua led into Israel: "And that generation was also gathered to their fathers" (Judg. 2.10).

The metaphorical interpretation of the phrase "gathered to his ancestors" concerns the afterlife—in the afterlife people will be reunited with their family members, their people, their kin. But the idea of an afterlife was very much underdeveloped in the biblical period. The biblical underworld, though a physical place, was not likely to have evoked images of family reunions.

Instead the phrase must refer to the physical place of burial. These kings were buried in tombs where their ancestors were already interred. Tombs were often reopened and reused, a necessity if family members that did not die at the same time were to be buried together, and royal tombs were no exception. The case of Abraham, quoted above in full, is a perfect example of a person who was "gathered to his people" being physically placed in his family tomb.

The phrase also reflects the physical act of burial. The practice of disinterring the skeleton of a family member and gathering its bones into an ossuary, or bone repository, is eerily reminiscent of "gathering" to one's fathers. It is more than likely that the biblical phrase was an oblique reference to the practice of placing bones in a pit or in an ossuary within the family tomb.

Another expression, similar to the phrase "gathered to his

fathers," substitutes the word "sleep" for "gather." It occurs when King David dies:

> Then David slept with his fathers. (1 Kings 2.10)

and again when other kings die:

> And Uzziah slept with his fathers and they buried him with his fathers in the burial field which belonged to the kings. (2 Chron. 26.23)
>
> And Ahaz slept with his fathers and they buried him in the city. (2 Chron. 29.27)
>
> And Omri slept with his fathers, and was buried in Samaria. (1 Kings 17.28)
>
> And Hezekiah slept with his fathers. (2 Kings 20.22)

There are many other such similar references.

The word "sleep" is used only for kings who died natural deaths, while the more stark "and he died" is used for kings who died violently. One of the more famous examples of this occurs with the death of King Josiah. Even though Josiah was a particularly beloved king, the phrase "and he died" was used because he died a violent death, killed in a battle against the Egyptians.

Euphemistic speech is not the only reason for this distinction in phraseology. The kings who died in battle could neither "sleep with" nor be "gathered to" their ancestors. They had to be buried where they fell, even if it was far from their ancestral tomb. Because embalming was never a tradition for the Israelites, bodies would not resist decomposition during transport. Anyone who died in the hot climate of Israel was therefore buried immediately, before decomposition could begin. The linguistic distinction reflects the physical reality of the burial places of these unfortunate kings who had to be buried right away, no matter where they were.[4]

These examples demonstrate another aspect of burial location in the biblical world. Family tombs were important, but appropriate locations of those tombs were equally important. Kings were generally buried within their capital cities or in cemeteries near their capital cities. Prophets were often buried near holy places.

Burial Markers

The custom of marking graves is widespread today but was used only within strict limits in the world of the Bible. Although archaeology usually offers convincing evidence, in the case of burial markers we can learn more from the Bible. Using archaeology alone, we would have to conclude that all graves were unmarked.

Of course some graves were easily visible, at least for a while. If a grave was in a still-active cemetery or if the grave itself was a family tomb that would be reused several years later, the top of its stone-capped shaft would stick out of the ground, and family members would remember exactly where to find it. Once a cemetery went out of use, however, dirt and grass would often cover the tomb shafts. While the area would not be intentionally built or farmed over, once local memory forgot it, it was gone.

The same pattern holds for tombs under the floors of houses. As long as the houses were occupied, the tombs were remembered and visible, but once the houses went out of use, the graves would be forgotten, an invisible part of the rubble.

While individuals are important today, the family as a whole was important then. Today we inscribe a person's name, date of birth, and date of death on almost every tombstone. In the biblical world individuals were subsumed by the family they belonged to, and often their very bones were mixed into a pile of ancestral bones in the center of the tomb.

The location of the family tomb was remembered for many generations. A person who was gathered to his ancestors and buried in a family tomb would not be lost. Some cemeteries in ancient Israel were used for hundreds of years at a time. Other cemeteries went out of use but became active again after a gap of several generations. Burial in a family tomb associated an individual with the greatness of his ancestors who were also buried there, and that was more important than future generations remembering his individual name or when he lived.

By the late biblical period, we begin to find coffins for individual burial. Later still, we find ossuaries. Coffins and ossuaries both preserve the individuality of the remains. The use of coffins triples during the course of the Iron Age, and ossuary burials gradually become popular during the Second Temple period.[5] It is possible that, influenced by the Persians, Greeks, and Romans who ruled them, the Jews began to desire personal recognition more than family continuity.

When the Bible mentions a burial marker, it is almost always for an atypical burial. For instance, a pile of stones was sometimes placed over the grave of a sinner or that of a fallen enemy.

> And they raised over him a great heap of stones that remains to this day; then the Lord turned from his burning anger. (Josh. 7.26)

> And [Joshua] hanged the king of Ai on a tree until evening; and at the going down of the sun Joshua commanded, and they took his body down from the tree, and cast it at the entrance of the gate of the city, and raised over it a great heap of stones, which stands there to this day. (Josh. 8.29)

> And they hung upon trees until evening. But at the time of the going down of the sun, Joshua commanded, and they took them down from the trees, and threw them into the cave . . . and they set great stones against the mouth of the cave, which remain to this very day. (Josh. 10.27)

> But at the time of the going down of the sun, Joshua commanded, and they took them down from the trees, and threw them into the cave where they had hidden themselves, and they set great stones against the mouth of the cave, which remain to this very day. (Josh. 11.27)

> And they took Absalom, and threw him into a great pit in the forest, and raised over him a very great heap of stones. (2 Sam. 18.17)

The fact that sinners and enemies received not only burials but marked burials attests to the extreme importance of proper burial in the culture of the Israelites. Not being buried was a fate worse than death itself. It is also possible that marking the graves of undesirables was intended as a substitute for the post-burial care and feeding of the dead that more acceptable members of society would receive after death.[6] Instead of actively remembering the person by performing rituals at the grave, the marker served as a passive way to signify a burial.

Another type of burial marker recorded in the Bible is a living tree, often an oak. More specifically, the body would be buried at the foot of a grown tree as opposed to planting a new tree near the grave. Tree burial was sometimes done when a person died away from home, presumably so that the location of the roadside grave would not be forgotten.

> And Deborah, Rebekah's nurse, died, and she was buried under an oak below Bethel; so the name of it was called Allon-bacuth [the Oak of Weeping]. (Gen. 35.8)

> But when the inhabitants of Jabesh-Gilead heard what the Philistines had done to Saul, all the valiant men arose, and went all night, and took the body of Saul and the bodies of his sons form the wall of Beth-Shan; and they came to Jabesh and burnt them there. And they took their bones and buried them under the tamarisk tree in Jabesh, and fasted seven days. (1 Sam. 31.11–13)

This latter passage not only describes burial under a tree, in this case a tamarisk, but also describes a cremation. The reason for the cremation—an unusual choice in the biblical world—was to protect the dignity of the deceased king. Saul's body and those of his sons had been humiliated by the Philistines; death had not been punishment enough. The Philistines had decapitated Saul after his death and hung his body on the walls of their city for all to see. The Jabesh-Gileadite rescuers cremated the bodies in order to give them back the dignity the Philistines had tried to take.

The reasons for burial under trees are many. One explanation is that trees were sometimes the locus of cultic activities such as sacrifices and as such may have been seen as appropriate for burial. But the more satisfactory explanation for burial near trees goes beyond vague cultic significance. As a representation of life, trees give solace for a loss. An analogous custom has arisen in modern times, since the formation of the modern State of Israel—Jews now plant trees in Israel in honor of someone who has died (as well as in honor of other life-cycle events such as births).

Yet the significance of trees for burial went further still. Interring a body under a tree is more than a symbolic act. Trees need water and soil to grow and thrive. A decomposing body gives the soil the nutrients that a tree needs to live. In the most literal sense, a death can turn into new life if the body is placed under a tree. It is quite possible that the Israelites, a people who were clearly not squeamish about the physicality of death, may have had this reason in mind.

Besides piles of stones and trees, a few burial markers mentioned in the Bible resemble our modern idea of tombstones. These are pillars erected on the grave after burial.

> So Rachel died, and she was buried on the way to Ephrath, that is, Bethlehem, and Jacob set up a pillar upon her grave; it is the pillar of Rachel's tomb, which is there to this day. (Gen. 35.19–20)

> Then (Josiah) said, "What is yonder monument that I see?" And the men of the city told him, "It is the tomb of the man of God who came from Judah and predicted these things which you have done against the altar at Bethel." And he said, "Let him be, let no man move his bones." (2 Kings 23.17–18)

Besides these references to pillars over graves, the Bible mentions other pillars, not specifically associated with graves, that served as memorials. One of these is a pillar that Absalom, King David's renegade son, erected for himself some time before his death, because he did not have a son to remember his name (2 Sam. 18.18).

Kings may have received a more individualized burial treatment than other people. Although it was found out of context, the Israel Museum in Jerusalem houses a square piece of stone inscribed with the following words: "Hither were brought the bones of Uzziah, King of Judah. Do not open!" Similar inscriptions have been found from the Second Temple period, though this is the only one that mentions a name of a biblical king.

Uzziah ruled in the eighth century B.C.E. The script of the

inscription, however, dates to the first century, meaning that this stone represents the later reburial of Uzziah. But in order for his bones to be preserved and reburied, Uzziah's original tomb would have had to be marked.

Whether or not a grave was marked by a monument, it is clear that family members remembered the locations of their ancestors and performed postmortem activities in the vicinity of the tombs. The dead were fed with sacrifices, sometimes even with food that was supposed to be reserved for the Temple. They were consulted and most likely worshipped at the site of burial.

Descriptions of Tombs and Burials

The Bible rarely gives detailed descriptions of ceremonies and physical places related to death or to any other part of religious culture. This is because such things were commonalities, part of a frame of reference known to everyone in ancient Israel. To describe a burial cave or a funeral in detail would have been the ancient equivalent of describing the White House to a modern American, instead of merely referring to it in passing.

In spite of this, the Bible contains sporadic descriptions of funeral rites, including those of burial.

When King Asa dies, the Bible describes it in the following manner:

> They laid [Asa] on a bier which had been filled with various kinds of spices prepared by the perfumer's art; and they made a very great fire in his honor. (2 Chron. 16.14)

This passage illustrates that kings were buried with spices, almost certainly because of their pleasant scent. Disguising the odor associated with a corpse would have been a prime concern in the hot climate of ancient Israel.

The text also mentions that a fire was made for the dead king. Neither the burning of a sacrifice nor any sort of cremation is mentioned, although both of those possibilities have been suggested. In fact the point of this fire is unclear.[7] Perhaps this was a ritual reserved for the funerals of kings. Or perhaps it was common at many funerals.

Biblical Imagery of Death

How did the Israelites view death itself? Biblical death imagery shows more than one view of death, but fear is the most evident of these. Biblical poetry contains metaphors and similes that liken death to dangerous, uncontrollable animals such as bulls, lions, and vicious dogs.

> Many bulls encompass me . . . they open their mouths at me like a ravening and roaring lion. . . . Yea, dogs are round about me; a company of evildoers encircle me. . . . Deliver my soul from the sword, my life from the power of the dog! Save me from the mouth of the lion, my afflicted soul from the horns of the wild oxen. (Ps. 22.12–22)

These images are frightening—death was a frightening thing. People thought of it as fierce and painful and uncontrollable. Furthermore, once dead you were cut off from God's grace.

Biblical poetry describes She'ol, the underworld where the dead go, in the following terms:

> I am reckoned among those who go down to the Pit; I am a man who has no strength, like one forsaken among the dead, like the slain that lie in the grave, like those whom thou dost remember no more, for they are cut off from thy hand. (Ps. 88.4–5)

If God does not remember the dead, clearly being dead was not desirable. This attitude vividly underscores the need for death rites—if God does not take care of the dead, it is up to their family members to do so, placing them in family tombs and tending those tombs in specific ways.

In looking at death customs from the ground up, as it were, we have considered the evidence, described it, and explained it. Now we must place biblical death practices into their larger historical and religious contexts, contexts that defined the identity of the Israelites. Israelite death practices evolved out of a Canaanite Cult of the Dead, a cult that was long-lived and that threatened not only the monarchy of Israel but the foundations of Israelite monotheism.

2

The Cult of the Dead in Ancient Israel

In using the term "cult" in discussions of the ancient world, we do not mean it in the modern, pejorative sense, the way some may refer to the cults of Jews for Jesus, Jonestown, or Heaven's Gate. In the ancient world cults were a regular, harmless part of the religious landscape—official religions often existed side by side with unofficial cults.

There were several such cults in the biblical world. Israelite women participated in active fertility cults, and many Israelites participated in the cults of various gods and goddesses that they were not supposed to be worshipping, such as Ba'al and Asherah.

The Cult of the Dead was probably one of the most active domestic cults of the biblical period, more active than the above-mentioned examples. It survived from the Bronze Age Canaanite period, into the Israelite period, and beyond. Its origins are even earlier, stretching far back into prehistory. The official religion of Israel tried to eradicate the Cult of the Dead, but it persisted in spite of this strong opposition.

At the end of the reign of King Saul, first king of the United Monarchy, the Cult of the Dead first became a political issue. Saul breaks a law that he himself enacted, a law that prohibited contact with the dead, in an attempt to change his personal fate.

Saul had always been a problematic king. He ruled over a people that had formerly been divided into tribes. Whether one supports the biblical version of events, in which the obstreperous tribes of Israel beg the prophet Samuel for a real king no matter what problems may derive from kingship, or whether one prefers a more sociological reading of the Bible, in which scattered tribes eventually coalesce into a single unit when Saul conquers their territory, the end result is the same: an entity that had previously been tribal must adjust to the curtailments of a monarchy that was thrust upon them.[1]

The beginnings of the monarchy had a profound effect on Saul's reign, as he had continually to legitimate himself in the eyes of his subjects. Perhaps because of this, his reign began to fall apart halfway through, when David, Saul's famous slingshot-swinging, lyre-playing son-in-law, moves to the center of the action.

The biblical redactors took great care to portray King David as the best of the kings of Israel. In spite of their carefully woven web, they found themselves in a quandary with the person of David himself. How can David be the legitimate king if

Saul was already the legitimate king and they were not related by blood?

Clearly Saul was too important an historical personage to eliminate. Saul, after all, united the Israelites as a nation for the first time. The biblical text had to resort to a literary device to undo Saul's greatness: Saul is proclaimed insane, and David, his son-in-law (the next best thing to a son in terms of legitimacy), is given God's blessing to become king in his place.

But a careful reading of the text reveals the truth of the situation. Israel is trying to separate into its original tribal units—the monarchy is falling apart at the seams. Some groups, in the territory of David's family, back David, but he does not have unanimous support even there: the young usurper must team up with the hated Philistines in order to find a strong army that will do as he commands. David later turns his back on the Philistines when he finds it convenient.

While David desperately tries to gain the support of the tribes, other sections of Israel back a surviving son of Saul as the legitimate heir to the throne.

This tension between unity and divisiveness is one of the ongoing themes of the monarchy of Israel. Even Solomon, considered the greatest king of the United Monarchy, encounters the problem and gerrymanders the tribal territories in a short-sighted attempt at solving it.

In the reign of Saul himself, we see the seeds of troubles ahead. Saul runs from David, no longer supported by all of his subjects.

Until this point in biblical history, the Cult of the Dead had been taken for granted. It had been a silent ritualistic backdrop for the stories of the patriarchs and the stories of Moses and the Exodus. With Saul's fall from grace it suddenly became an issue.

One of the reasons why the tribes begged for a king, for Saul, was that they wished to be like all the other nations (1 Sam. 8.5). At the same time Israel as a whole constantly fought against being like all the other nations. They were the only nation that was monotheistic, choosing Yahweh, a god previously worshipped in only a small region of the South, as their one and only god. They were the only nation that observed laws that limited what they could eat, and they were the only one that practiced ritual circumcision on male infants.[2]

While they were unlike any other peoples in these ways, the only peoples that they encountered regularly—the only groups that mattered—were the Canaanites and the Philistines. Their daily cultural contact with the Canaanites gave the Israelites a true identity crisis: when the Israelites stood next to the Canaanites their fundamental differences were all but invisible, because the Canaanites were so like them in many other ways.

The Canaanites and the Israelites eventually built houses and temples according to the same architectural principles. They most likely dressed in the same manner. They grew the same crops, ate most of the same foods, spoke dialects of the same language, responded to the same environmental and political threats, and especially buried and treated their dead in the same way.

As the leader of the Israelites, Saul had to work hard to preserve his people's fundamental differences in the face of so many similarities. Some of this fight was easy and obvious. Since monotheism was a major tenet of Israelite religion, the state officially objected to the worship of other gods. Throughout biblical history the Israelites would "backslide" and worship the Canaanite god Ba'al, or the Canaanite goddess Asherah. This sort of worship was not permitted by the very definition of monotheism and was against state law.

The imperative to react against the Canaanites was especially strong during Saul's problematic reign. Israel was barely unified, yet it was already straying, and Saul was losing his grip on his kingdom.

Toward the end of his life, Saul was not only threatened by David but also by his old enemy the Philistines. If the passages are read from a literary standpoint, one could say that Saul reacted to the pressures of the situations. Whatever his motivation, he turns to necromancy—the practice of calling up the dead and asking them for advice—as a last resort. The practice, a manifestation of the Canaanite Cult of the Dead, was clearly outlawed in Israelite practice.

One of the commandments in Exodus that follows the original ten is, "Thou shall not permit a witch to live" (Exod. 22.18). The main role of witches in the biblical world was to engage in necromancy. This commandment is repeated and expanded in other places as well, including Deuteronomy:

> There shall not be found among you any one who . . . practices divination, a soothsayer or an augur, or a sorcerer, or a charmer, or a medium, or a wizard, or a necromancer. (Deut. 18.10–11)

Punishment for breaking this injunction is stated clearly in Leviticus:

> If a person turns to mediums and wizards . . . I [God] will set my face against that person, and will cut him off from among his people. (Lev. 20.6)

> A man or a woman who is a medium or a wizard shall be put to death; they shall be stoned with stones, their blood shall be upon them. (Lev. 20.27)

These were quite serious punishments, even in the strict climate of the biblical world. Being cut off from the community was considered a fate equal to death, and being stoned was a very unpleasant way to die.

According to 1 Sam. 28.8–9, King Saul himself reiterated these very laws. In spite of this, he seeks the help of a witch. He is engaged in battle with the Philistines, part of the war that eventually claimed his life. He is losing and desperate, and views necromancy as his last hope. Believing that God will not talk to him directly anymore because He has turned away from him, he wants advice from someone close to God.

Saul looks to Samuel for this, the prophet who led Israel before he became king. Unfortunately Samuel is already dead, and the only way Saul can reach him is by finding a witch. But witches were afraid for their lives. Because of the laws quoted above, no one would admit to being a witch, much less perform an act of necromancy for the King of Israel—such a request might be a trick that would lead to punishment and death.

Nonetheless Saul finds a woman known as a witch. He finds her in the town of En Dor, just over the mountains from Beth Shean, where he is fighting the Philistines.[3] He disguises himself and asks her to call up the spirit of Samuel. She refuses, citing fear of the king's law, not knowing that the king himself is standing in front of her. Saul, still disguised, promises that nothing will happen to her. She eventually obliges and calls up Samuel's ghost. At this point the witch realizes that she is dealing with Saul himself.

The apparition of Samuel is angry and asks Saul, "Why have you disturbed me by bringing me up?" (1 Sam. 28.15). Samuel then criticizes Saul, reiterating that God has abandoned him, then predicts his death and the death of his sons in battle the next day (1 Sam. 28.6–25).

While the motivation for this story is to cast Saul in a poor light, the real moral of the story for an ancient Israelite reader is that necromancy works—the witch really did call up Samuel's spirit. If the possibility of successful calling of the dead was taken as a given in ancient Israel, why was it considered so wrong? Why was necromancy against the law when even the king himself resorted to it? Was there something wrong with using dead people to predict the future, and if so, was the problem with knowing the future, or with the act of consulting the dead in the first place?

It seems that knowing the future was not the problem. Communicating with the dead, which was seen as a real possibility if the story of the witch of En Dor is any indication, was.

The ultimate goal of the Cult of the Dead was to keep the doors of communication open between the realm of the living and the realm of the dead. Stated in a slightly different way, the goal of this cult was to make the already extant relationship between living and dead a positive one for the living. Either way, the Israelite community considered communicating with the dead necessary, whether out of fear of revenge—for not fulfilling their familial obligations to the dead—or out of the desire to seek their advice, as they were thought to know all.

The ultimate goal of the United Monarchy of Israel, under Saul as well as under David and Solomon, was to keep the people united as a single nation, in spite of their tendency to revert to tribal divisions in hard times. This goal of unity went directly against the goals and practical activities of the Cult of the Dead.

The Cult of the Dead was family oriented. One would not sacrifice to or ask advice from someone else's dead ancestors, only from one's own dead ancestors. A person would maintain the tomb of his father, his grandfather, and perhaps his extended family members as well, if no direct descendants of uncles and cousins survived. There are many references in the Bible, as well as in texts from neighboring Syria, to the son being responsible for upkeep of the father's tomb, as well as for the father's funeral. The son was also responsible for maintaining his father's ancestor cult.

Beyond the family level was the clan level. Ancestor cults could survive extremely long periods of time if several related families of cousins all maintained the cult of their common great- or great-great-grandfather.

And beyond the clan level was the tribal level. Several clans belonged to each tribe, and within the tribe, each clan would maintain the cults of its own ancestors. The Cult of the Dead was probably integral to the way the tribe held itself together—each clan within the tribe had its own ancestral tombs, and each clan maintained its own ancestral cults separately, but simultaneously. Clans were distinct and separate entities but were simultaneously bound together by common ancient ancestors. This attachment to ancestors, ancient and recent, held the entire tribe together.

In these ways ancestor worship, or the Cult of the Dead, bound clans and tribes into cohesive units. Tribes as well as clans were kin-oriented, and the ancestor cult was a visible, always current expression of kin ties.

This natural cohesion of tribal units was in direct opposition to the goals of Israel as a single political state. Citizens of the state needed to exchange their tribal loyalties for the greater good of the kingdom, or else the entire kingdom would be threatened. Without loyalty to the central authority, the king would not be able to effectively lead an army, or organize public works projects, or show a united front to an enemy. Tribal and clan ties undermined the centrality of the monarchy, always threatening to break it into its original tribal units.

The Cult of the Dead was the strongest surviving vestige of the original clan and tribal ties of Israel. It was why King Solomon gerrymandered the tribal territories (1 Kings 4), hoping to break down the tribal loyalties of the people. Once he did this he was able significantly to reinforce his army (1 Kings 10.26). Even Solomon's success in uniting and strengthening Israel as a single entity was limited only to his own lifetime, as civil war broke out immediately following his death. The northern tribes fought the southern ones, and eventually the two separate political entities of the Divided Monarchy arose from the chaos.

At the end of the eighth century B.C.E., after the fall of the northern kingdom of Israel to the Assyrians, the government of Judah intensified its objections to the Cult of the Dead. Judah at that time was also in danger of being destroyed, and therefore had a sudden and intense need to bolster its defense.

The Judahite prophet Isaiah spelled out the politics of the time in religious terms—God allowed the Assyrians to conquer Israel as a punishment for Israel's sinful nature. The same thing would happen to Judah, Isaiah threatened, if the Judahites continued in their sinful ways. Isaiah and contemporary biblical writers called for a halt to all non-Yahwist worship, including the cults of the old Canaanite deities, and especially the Cult of the Dead:

> I (God) spread out my hands . . . to a rebellious people who walk in a way that is not good, following their own devices . . . who sit in tombs and spend the night in secret places; who eat swine's flesh and broth of abominable things is in their vessels. . . . Behold . . . I will not keep silent, but I will repay, yea, I will repay. (Isa. 65.2–6)

Isaiah equates sitting in tombs, that is, taking part in rituals associated with the Cult of the Dead, with the worst kinds of sins, such as eating forbidden foods. He says that God will punish Judahites who act in this way. The punishment, spelled out in poetic terms here as well as elsewhere, is destruction by the same northern peoples that destroyed Israel. Isaiah allows for redemption, but only if Judah mends its ways. Clearly the ancient Cult of the Dead was hurtful to the official religion of the eighth century, at least in the eyes of its prophets.

The Cult of the Dead was dangerous to Israel for another reason as well. Not only did it threaten the unity of Israel, it also erased the differences between the monotheistic Israelites and the polytheistic Canaanites. The Israelites (and Judahites) practiced this cult exactly as the Canaanites did. This was a problem for the Judahite redactors because the Canaanites are criticized scathingly throughout the biblical narratives. The Israelites understood that Yahweh was the only God—surely they would not emulate the cultic practices of the hated, polytheistic Canaanites!

In reality the Israelites practiced the Cult of the Dead exactly as the Canaanites did. In fact the similarity of practice is one of the strongest hints of the intertwined history of the two groups.

The Canaanites had a strong Cult of the Dead with a long history. Hundreds of years before the Israelites arrived on the scene, the Canaanites buried their dead under the floors of their homes. They also buried them in family-based cemeteries, included objects for their use and enjoyment in their tombs, and maintained sacrificial cults in their honor. The Cult of the Dead in Canaan did not significantly change its character for hundreds of years, and even the coming of the Israelites did not alter it. The Israelites, whether they originated from the midst of the Canaanites, came out of the southern desert, or a combination of both, followed the Canaanite Cult of the Dead to the letter.

Examinations of the tombs of Israelites and Canaanites reveal that both peoples used the same types of locations for burial and included the same types of objects. The many biblical prohibitions against the Cult of the Dead, some of which were quoted above, also serve as evidence for the cult's staying power. Other biblical passages do not criticize the Cult of the Dead. Instead they tacitly acknowledge the cult's existence within Israel, even though they do not approve of it.

For most of Israelite history, the religious administrators of the United Monarchy understood that the Cult of the Dead was too strong to abolish. They tried only to rein it in, to limit the ways in which one could practice it:

> Then you shall say before the Lord your God, "I have not eaten of the tithe while I was mourning . . . or offered any of it to the dead." (Deut. 26.13–14)

Tithed food was food that all farmers had to reserve from their crops to give to the priesthood as their living—the taxation of the day. There was more than one tithe, and both biblical and rabbinic laws are very explicit about how they must be reserved.

Because this food was clearly special, a practice had developed of taking it and giving it to one's dead ancestors. The Israelites' desire to appease and please their dead by giving them the best food available was irresistible.

The first part of the biblical prohibition quoted here—not to eat from tithed food oneself while in mourning—stems from the fact that offerings to the dead were rarely wasted in the ancient world; people recognized that the dead would not actually eat offerings left at their tombs, that this food would be eaten by animals or rot, so they ate it themselves.

The aforementioned law was a small prohibition specifically directed at a particular custom. It was not intended to end the Cult of the Dead itself, since ending it was not considered possible for most of Israelite history.

The Cult of the Dead involved more than the placement and feeding of the dead. Beyond this, the living engaged in specific annual and family sacrifices for the dead. We know of these sacrifices from a number of sources, but mainly from the book of Samuel.

> And the man Elkanah and all his house went up to offer to the Lord the yearly sacrifice. (1 Sam. 1.21)

> . . . when she went up with her husband to offer the yearly sacrifice. (1 Sam. 2.19)

> . . . then say, "David earnestly asked leave of me to run to Bethlehem his city; for there is a yearly sacrifice there for all the family." (1 Sam. 20.6)

The last of these references equates the yearly sacrifice with a family sacrifice, and other references also speak about a family sacrifice.

> And he said, 'Let me go; for our family holds a sacrifice in the city, and my brother has commanded me to be there.' (1 Sam. 20.29)

None of the above references say specifically that these annual family sacrifices were for the ancestors, as part of the Cult of the Dead, but there is reason to believe that is exactly what they were.[4] Mesopotamian texts tell about a ceremony known as the

Kispu. During the Kispu, family members would present food offerings as well as libations to their deceased ancestors, as well as utter their names. The Kispu would be performed monthly—as opposed to yearly—and family members practiced it to placate the spirits of the deceased and to win their favor. Another Mesopotamian ceremony, the Paqidum, was also an occasion to feed and water the dead.

An indisputable reference to sacrifices to the dead occurs in Ps. 106.28:

> Then they . . . ate sacrifices to the dead.

It is more than likely that the biblical family sacrifices were not performed at a random time of year but rather on the anniversary of the person's death.

In the Rabbinic period the anniversary of a person's death was still celebrated, though no longer by sacrificing. This annual remembrance has passed down into modern Judaism in the form of a candle left burning for the entire anniversary day, and recitations of special mourners' prayers. In this sense modern Jews still practice the ancient Cult of the Dead.

Beyond leaving food and objects in the tombs, and beyond annual sacrifices, other aspects of the Cult of the Dead included occasional practices, rather than ones fixed in time. A person would occasionally ask the dead for advice or for predictions of the future, as Saul asked Samuel. And occasionally the dead would demonstrate their power to heal or to revive other dead.

The powers of healing and knowing the future are both powers that the Bible more usually attributes to Yahweh, and herein lies a huge problem. If the dead possess the same powers as Yahweh, and if people sacrifice to the dead just as they sacrifice to Yahweh, the dead may be godlike in some respects.

This problem was fundamental to the biblical redactors, especially in the context of the late-eighth-century religious reforms. Judahite Yahwism called for the worship of Yahweh alone, to the exclusion of any other gods, yet the Judahites persisted in treating their dead as they treated Yahweh. In the eyes of the prophets of Judah, the Cult of the Dead actually put Yahweh's preeminence into question and, worse yet, gave Yahweh competition from many mini-gods.

Here was yet another reason for the biblical proscriptions against the Cult of the Dead. Strictest monotheism would not permit a Cult of the Dead. And because the Cult of the Dead persisted throughout the Israelite period, strictest monotheism was never fully practiced or enforced.

Many aspects of Israel's Cult of the Dead were not only shared with the Canaanites, they actually predated them. The fear of death, and the fear of the dead, were some of the deepest, longest, and most consistently expressed cultural aspects of the land of the Bible.

3

A History of Death in the Land of the Bible

One of the most interesting questions about the archaeology and history of ancient Israel is also one of the hardest to answer. The question concerns the transitions from one period to the next. This issue is deeply related to that of burial practices and the Cult of the Dead. In the cases where an unrelated, usurping people replace an existing culture, unrelated religious traditions, including burial traditions, should be evident. A conquering culture may even go so far as to destroy the religious institutions of the preceding culture out of pride or hatred, or both.

If, on the other hand, one culture develops out of another, religious traditions, including burial traditions, should pass down almost unchanged from one to the next.

A period-by-period examination of burial practices in ancient Israel makes one fact very clear: little about burial practices changed after the Middle Bronze Age—traditions survived intact from 2000 B.C.E. through to the end of antiquity and beyond. An argument can even be made that the progression begins earlier than that, with Early Bronze Age practices, and it is even possible that some of the phrases that the Bible uses for life and death echo beliefs that go back to the Chalcolithic period, some six thousand years ago.

After a few "false starts," death practices remained startlingly consistent over much time and cultural disruption. The changes that are seen are often variations on a theme.

Before looking at the changes in burial rituals over the years, it is best to describe the features that most burials of the biblical world shared, beginning to end.

The first item shared by almost all tombs in ancient Israel is tomb offerings. The tomb offerings are consistent throughout the periods discussed, especially in the Bronze and Iron Ages (as opposed to the prehistoric periods). Common offerings included drinks such as wine, beer, and water, left in large jars and jugs. Grains, cereals, and meats were left on open platters and in bowls. Oils and unguents were placed in smaller juglets and jars. These items were generally left close to the body, most commonly near the head, waist, or feet. Sometimes they were left in a corner of the tomb.

Nonedible items are just as common in tombs as edible ones. These included weapons such as swords, arrows, and spears; tools such as axes, adzes, and knives; expensive furniture such as tables and chairs inlaid with ivory or bone; jewelry of all sorts; other decorative items of stones and precious stones; and bronze, silver, and gold statuettes and figurines.

While the ceramic styles changed from period to period—a Middle Bronze Age water jug is easily distinguished from an Iron Age one—a jug is still a jug, no matter what the details of its shape. Certainly there were variations in how much of each item was left in each period—burials of some periods contain high proportions of food and necessities, while burials of other periods contain higher proportions of luxury items—but the motivation to leave food and drink, as well as items of prestige, remained intact through the centuries. Variations in the proportions of food and jewelry reflect the history and economy of any given period.

One explanation for the presence of funerary offerings is that they were intended for use in the afterlife. Individuals would need to eat in the next world just as they would in this world, and they might need their tools and weapons as well. According to this explanation, tomb inclusions were for practical purposes that benefited the deceased.

Another possible explanation for leaving funerary offerings is that they were presents for the deceased. Clearly the relatively small amount of food that fits in a tomb is not enough to last forever. The survivors must have recognized this. If so, the tomb items may have been intended as presents, initial tokens of esteem for the newly dead, to be followed by later expressions of ancestor worship such as sacrifices and prayers.

It is difficult to know the intent behind tomb offerings.[1] They may have been intended for use in the afterworld, or they may have been presents, or they may have been items that were too painful to keep yet impossible to throw out. Modern examples of the latter include teddy bears being placed in tombs with children who have died, and squeeze toys placed in graves in pet cemeteries.

What follows is a brief overview of the death practices of the land of Israel from prehistory to the Roman period.

The Neolithic Period (9000–4500 B.C.E.)

On the last day of the 1953 excavation season of the site of ancient Jericho, Dame Kathleen Kenyon broke the primary rule of field excavation. This preeminent British archaeologist simply reached into the wall of dirt that separated one excavation trench from the other and pulled something out. She did not measure or record, and she did not use the proper tools but she was fortunate enough to pull out a skull.

It was not just any skull. This one could stare back at her. It had eyes of inlaid shell and cheeks of carefully chiseled plaster. It looked human. Or partly human, since the lower part of the face was missing. The lower jaw had fallen off, and the perfect human face stopped just below its perfect row of top teeth.

The lack of a lower jaw instantly gave Kenyon a clue about how long after death this ritual plastering had been done. Since the lower jaw of a human skull is not connected to the upper jaw by bone but only by muscle and sinews, Kenyon knew that a year or two had passed between the person's death and his ritual plastering—the length of time it takes for flesh to decay. Once the flesh had decayed and only the bones were left someone easily removed the skull from the rest of the body and plastered it to make it look alive.

But where was the rest of the body? Kenyon's team went back to work and soon found more plastered skulls in buildings, but still no skeletons. Finally they found the cemetery of Jericho. Each tomb space of the cemetery had many bodies laid out, each with offerings typical of the Neolithic period. As expected, the upper parts of the skulls were missing from many of the skeletons. When other archaeologists began to dig Neolithic sites elsewhere in Israel and Syria, similar skulls and headless bodies were found. Later, at other sites, other archaeologists began to find similar skulls, some with lower jaws intact, some with their mouths and teeth completely plastered over.

Neolithic communities probably brought these skulls "back to life" ritualistically as a form of ancestor worship, and probably did so only to select elders of the communities. It is likely that the people of the Neolithic culture believed that the head was the center of the soul (not of intelligence), therefore they saved the heads of those elders who were the most effective community leaders so that they could continue to dispense advice after death and into eternity.

This is the earliest concrete evidence for ancestor worship from the land of Israel. Ancestor worship continues in almost every period from the Neolithic forward. The line is jagged, however, as the types of evidence for ancestor worship change frequently, especially in the early periods. The Neolithic period, for instance, is the only period in which people plastered the skulls of their ancestors back to life, but that does not mean that the concept of ancestor worship was born anew each time—just the opposite is true. Even when a particular expression of ancestor worship was abandoned, the general concept held fast.

The Neolithic period spans 4,500 years altogether. The tradition of skull plastering lasted throughout most of this time. This tradition also stretched over hundreds of miles of territory, from southern Israel to northern Syria.

Certainly some differences in burial treatment exist from the beginning to the end of this long period, but they are minor ones. Bodies from all subperiods within the Neolithic were almost always buried in a flexed or semi-flexed position, something like the fetal position. This is not unusual. Flexed burial positions are known from some of the earliest burials ever found, from the Natufian period, which precedes the Neolithic by several thousand years, and even from the Paleothic period that begins human history.

The flexed bodies of Neolithic Jericho were often placed on woven mats. Skulls were removed and placed in pits in all parts of the period, but in the earlier part of it they were not plastered over. Plastering seems to have begun in the middle of the period, what is known as the Pre-Pottery Neolithic B.

Another phenomenon of the Jericho skulls is that some show evidence of skull deformation.[2] This suggests that some of the residents of Jericho had their heads wrapped tightly with a cloth for long periods at an early stage of the development of this practice. This type of ritualistic deformation is also known from other Neolithic sites.

But the skulls are not the only evidence for ancestor worship in the Neolithic period. Archaeologists have found a number of stone masks from sites in Israel and Syria. These masks eerily resemble the plastered skulls. Like the skulls, they have empty eye sockets, no nose (the skulls have poorly re-formed plaster noses), and oddly emphasized, rather jagged teeth. In some sense the masks look more like skulls than the skulls themselves. Perhaps this reflects a ritual significance of the skull itself, rather than the head.

Perhaps the skulls, and also the masks in lieu of skulls, were held up or carried in a funerary ceremony. One might carry such a skull during the funeral of another family member or perhaps during another ceremony concerning ancestor worship, outside of burial. There is no better way to call on one's ancestors for assistance than by parading their own skulls around, in a way becoming them by holding them up ceremonially, or wearing the representational masks.

The Chalcolithic Period (4500–3200 B.C.E.)

The Neolithic period gave way to the Chalcolithic in the middle of the fifth millennium B.C.E. The new culture was vastly different from the old one, and even the burial practices show complete discontinuity. Never has there been a sharper break between two traditions. The unusual plastered skulls of the Neolithic period disappeared suddenly, never to be repeated, and were replaced by a Chalcolithic burial tradition that was just as unusual.

> Then the Lord God formed man of the dust of the ground, and breathed into his nostrils the breath of life; and man became a living soul. (Gen. 2.7)

This passage of Genesis is the first of many biblical references to the "breath of life." According to biblical texts, God's breath has the power to change inanimate dust into a living being with a soul and a consciousness. Israelite burial practices do not reflect this belief in any concrete, physical way, but in the Chalcolithic period, some three thousand years before the time of the Israelites, the "breath of life" is evident in practices relating to death.

In the Chalcolithic, people regularly practiced secondary burial, disinterring their dead after a year or two, collecting all the long, portable bones, and placing them in clay ossuaries or bone repositories. The ossuaries would then be buried in a cemetery.

Ossuaries are not common in the ancient world. Chalcolithic ossuaries, however, have one feature that sets them apart from all later ossuaries and that also links them to the biblical passage quoted above. Chalcolithic ossuaries have large human noses.

These noses are made of clay and are applied to the upper regions of the container, often between two small, painted eyes. The noses are well out of proportion to the eyes, in fact they are the most prominent features of the ossuaries.

There is no functional reason to have a nose-shaped protuberance (or one of any other shape) on these objects. Since the noses do not have a practical function, they most likely had a ritual function. It is only a small leap to connect them to the "breath of life."

According to the biblical passage, God gave life to the inanimate shape of man by breathing his own breath into him. The reverse of this takes place when man dies—God's breath leaves him. With this in mind, it is easy to see why ossuaries might have noses. God's breath is no longer in the bones of man, so in order to enable man to exist, or "live" in the afterlife, a nose is attached to his ossuary, either representing the nose/breath of God or in lieu of God's breath.

A slightly different interpretation is that the noses represent the breath of life of the individual before death. His life force, or soul, needed to be preserved alongside his earthly remains, and the preservation of the soul along with the body took the shape of the clay nose.

Noses appear in one other place in the Chalcolithic period. Chalcolithic offering stands made of basalt are a common item in the northern part of the country, specifically in the Golan Heights, a fair distance from the epicenter of the ossuary finds, which are in the vicinity of modern Tel Aviv. These stands are approximately a foot tall and are shaped like small pillars. Their tops are rounded into a basin shape, and immediately below this basin a schematic head is carved out, sometimes with knobs for ears and eyes, but always with an extremely prominent nose.

Besides prominent noses and painted eyes, another feature of Chalcolithic ossuaries is their extremely unusual shape. Chalcolithic ossuaries are shaped like miniature houses—houses with noses. Many of them have vegetative patterns drawn all over their fronts and sides—reeds tied into bundles to form columns, just the way the reed huts of the time were actually constructed. The clay slabs that form the sides of the ossuary are usually punctuated with windows and doors. Sometimes the reed columns are even represented in clay. These architectural, domestic features appear to be as intrinsic to the ossuaries as are the noses, and give credence to the idea of tomb-as-home that is seen in the biblical period.

There were less unusual types of burial in the Chalcolithic period as well. Many burials in the southern part of the country, the Negev, consisted of plain pits surrounded by a circle of stones. Interestingly, circles of stones are mentioned in the Bible as a type of burial marker used for the graves of enemies (see Chapter 1). If the people of the Chalcolithic period can be viewed as "proto-Canaanites," this burial marker—like the "breath of life"—makes sense when read together with biblical texts. It is therefore possible that the Bible reflects not just one but two death rituals that go back very far in history.

The Early Bronze Age (3200–2000 B.C.E.)

At the hottest, driest part of the Dead Sea, there is a peninsula of land, and on this peninsula is an ancient site called Bab edh-Dhra. This site was occupied during the several stages of the Early Bronze Age and then abandoned.

The burials of Early Bronze Age Bab edh-Dhra are more memorable than its living areas. Archaeologists have called some of these burials "charnal houses." They consist of long, rectangular rooms filled with the bones of dozens of individuals. Strikingly, these rooms have evidence of fire everywhere. Were people cremating their dead in mass burials? Were they doing this in an attempt to prevent the spread of an infectious, fatal disease? Was it a religious ritual?

These questions cannot be answered adequately. Whatever

the reason, this type of treatment of the dead was never repeated in the land of the Bible. A more approachable question concerns where the people were living—here is a cemetery, with evidence for cremation, but there are no significant settlements in the vicinity.

The Bab edh-Dhra cemetery brings up a point that goes beyond just the Early Bronze Age. Not only is this cemetery removed from any settlements, it also contains secondary burials, that is, skeletons that someone dug up from another location and moved here.

The dead could not rest in peace if they were not buried in the right place. This is a clue to the mode of subsistence in the period as well as the beliefs about death and afterlife. If these people were semi-nomadic, they would live in more than one place and die in more than one place as well.

Many semi-nomadic groups lived on the fringes of society in the ancient world, regularly interacting with the sedentary populace. Many nomad groups were pastoralists, that is, they had flocks that needed grazing land. Often a group would stay in one camp for an entire summer season, grazing its flocks until nothing was left in the vicinity. When the grazing land was emptied and the rainy season came, the group would move to another pasture land, one with a new supply of food. As recently as the nineteenth century, nomadic groups would commonly return to their same winter and summer camps in the Middle East.

But these nomadic groups were nomads only because of their livelihood—they did not wander because they wanted to. The fact that they would reuse the same winter and summer camps (neither of which is necessarily visible in the archaeological record) attests to this. Like other groups, they had a burial ground for their clans and families, and like other groups, they believed it was important to be buried with ancestors.

This is probably why people practiced secondary burial. Digging up one's father's bones was not considered sacrilegious. If he died at the wrong camp, away from the ancestral cemetery, there was no choice—he had to be moved and reburied in the proper place.

The ancestral burial grounds were cemeteries like the one at Bab edh-Dhra. These were the places where people were, most literally, gathered to their ancestors. But why some of them were burned after they were transported back to camp is still a mystery.

Except for the Bab edh-Dhra charnal houses, the tombs of the rest of the period are not exceptional. In some ways the Early Bronze Age begins—and defines—typical Canaanite burial practices. The Early Bronze Age is the period in which we first see shaft-and-chamber tombs, sometimes called "caves" in the literature about the period, though they are really the same sort of carved chambers as in the Israelite period (a thousand years later), and all the periods in between.

The Intermediate Bronze Age (2200–2000 B.C.E.)

The tombs of the Intermediate Bronze Age have been given interesting names. At the site of Jericho there are dagger tombs, outsized tombs, and bead tombs, among others.

The Intermediate Bronze Age was a period of collapse. It is

filled with small-scale regional cultures, ones that look nothing like the cultures that preceded or followed it. In fact it took many years of research and study before the period could be accurately described.

One of the difficulties with the scholarship on the Intermediate Bronze Age is that for years many more cemeteries than settlement sites were known. For a long time, scholars were defining this period solely by its tombs. It was not until later that they discovered the small settlements and regional nature of the period.

At around 2200 B.C.E. the long-established urban society of the Early Bronze Age suddenly collapsed in on itself. Early Bronze Age cities lay desolate, squatters perching on their ruins. The reasons for this collapse are many. The environment was certainly a factor, as there may have been a climate change or a severe drought. The contemporary political collapse of Egypt was also most likely a factor, as the two countries were always linked together economically and often politically.

The squatters who occupied the ruins of Early Bronze Age cities, and other people who settled their own, new sites far from the ruined cities, comprise the populace of the Intermediate Bronze Age. The collapsed nature of the Intermediate Bronze Age is evident at every archaeological turn—even the pottery of the period is made up of squat, unattractive shapes that are clear deteriorations of elegant Early Bronze Age forms.

Obviously a major cultural shift had taken place. Yet the tombs of the Intermediate Bronze Age are very similar to the shaft-and-chamber tombs that were occasionally used in the Early Bronze Age. An entire society had fallen apart, yet the burial practices of the people carried on. This is one of the greatest proofs for the continuity of burial practices.

The most typical tomb type of the Intermediate Bronze Age was the shaft-and-chamber tomb. Much more commonly used then than in the Early Bronze Age, this tomb type was found throughout the country. It was not yet refined and standardized—that would take place in the Middle Bronze Age—but it was solidly part of Intermediate Bronze Age burial practices.

Kathleen Kenyon, the same archaeologist who pulled the Neolithic plastered skull out of a trench in Jericho, organized the Intermediate Bronze tombs of Jericho into several categories based on the shape of the tomb as well as what sort of offerings it contained.

Kenyon's "Dagger Tombs" not only had uniformly wide chambers, they all contained copper daggers that were styled alike. Her "Pottery Tombs" all had pottery types that may have been manufactured specifically for mortuary use—these shapes are not found in the settlement at all. Her "Outsize Tombs" were much larger and deeper than most others. Not all of her "Bead Tombs" actually contained beads—she also classified them based on shape and size.

But Kenyon might not have interpreted all the tomb evidence correctly. For instance, she believed that the "Pottery Tombs" were all secondary burials because they contained disarticulated skeletons. More likely, these skeletons were disarticulated due to later reuse of the tombs, when previous burials were pushed aside to make room for more recent ones, as was the custom. This in no way implies secondary burial.

Because of the larger number of Intermediate Bronze Age

tombs, several scholars have used the Jericho cemetery as a complete database in and of itself. In fact they have taken the very same material and come up with completely opposing results. Clearly the Jericho data can be interpreted in more than one way, which is one reason the tombs of the Intermediate Bronze Age, while interesting and comparatively well preserved, do not, in the end, help our understanding of the social situations of the period.[3]

The other type of burial structure associated with the Intermediate Bronze Age is at least as puzzling as the misinterpreted shaft-and-chamber tombs. These are dolmens—huge, aboveground structures of stone. They are found in several parts of the biblical world, especially in the Golan Heights and across the river in Jordan.

Beneath the round, masonry superstructure of a dolmen is a burial space. The space is most often round, in keeping with the roundness of the structure itself, and the floor is usually paved with cobblestones.

Not much else is known about these dolmen burials. As a rule they contain very little pottery and even less skeletal material. This is because they are so completely exposed, both to the elements and to tomb robbers. It is not known if one, two, or many individuals were placed in them. In most cases it is not clear when these dolmens were first built and used. It is likely that many of them were built in the Intermediate Bronze Age, but scholars have suggested other periods as well, such as the Chalcolithic period. Whenever they were built, most dolmens were reused in several periods.

The dolmens of the Golan Heights are found in clumps—

fields of dolmens. In most cases there are no large settlements nearby. Because so few bones remain in dolmens, it is not known whether they housed secondary burials.

Only one thing is clear about dolmens. They are large tomb monuments—larger, more imposing, and much more visible than any other sort of tomb in the country. Biblical-period tombs did not have traditional markers. Whoever was building dolmens wanted their tombs to be visible from miles away. This is unusual in ancient Israel. Perhaps it means that a different social or ethnic group built the dolmens. If so, they blended well into their adopted society, as there is no convincing trace of them in any other archaeological remains.

The Middle Bronze Age (2000–1500 B.C.E.)

If the Intermediate Bronze Age was a period of collapse, a nonurban interlude, the Middle Bronze Age is a period of reurbanization. In many ways the Middle Bronze Age heralds the true beginning of the social landscape described in the Bible. Cities are re-forming at the very beginning of the Middle Bronze Age, often on tells last populated in the Early Bronze Age and sometimes on completely new sites. New technologies came into the country in this period, such as the fast pottery wheel and new metallurgical techniques, both learned from neighbors on the coast of Syria, who had not experienced collapses in their social fabric.

While there are no further cultural breaks after the Middle Bronze Age, some major changes do take place—new peoples, such as the Israelites and the Philistines, enter the country; old peoples, such as the Canaanites, assimilate out of existence; foreign powers, such as Egypt and eventually Babylon, attack and rule; alliances are made and broken. From the Middle Bronze Age forward, all these changes are not only recorded in the historical records of the ancient Near East, they are also clear in the archaeological record. From the Middle Bronze Age forward, each culture is a natural continuation of the previous one.

But the burial practices of the Middle Bronze Age look similar to those of the Intermediate Bronze Age, a period with which it has little other connection. Middle Bronze burial practices look so similar to earlier ones because they are the same as the earlier ones—they survived in spite of the intervening collapse of society. Just as earlier burial traditions survived during the Intermediate Bronze Age, they continued after it as well. This proves how conservative burial practices can be and how firmly they resist change.

The people lost their cities in the Intermediate Bronze Age but not their ancestral memories. In the Middle Bronze Age, when they were able to reurbanize, they retained these ancient, ancestral burial traditions that had survived through the discontinuity of the earlier period.

The shafts of the tombs are smaller in the Middle Bronze Age than they were in the preceding Intermediate Bronze Age, and chambers are slightly smaller now too. The tomb structure is more uniform now, generally consisting of a single shaft plunging into the ground, ending in an open space that acted as a sort of courtyard. This subterranean courtyard in turn led to two or sometimes three chambers, spreading outward. These burial chambers were not always the same size, not even within the same tomb. Some were larger and some were smaller. Some contained single interments, and others contained double or even triple ones, but seldom more than that.

Sometimes Middle Bronze Age people actually reused Intermediate Bronze Age tombs to bury their own dead, pushing aside older skeletons and offerings to make room for the new interment. This reuse of much earlier tombs confirms the continuity of practice in death customs—the Middle Bronze Age people considered themselves the direct descendants of their nonurban predecessors, even continuing family burial caves begun by them.[4]

But Middle Bronze Age mortuary customs look forward as well as backward. Just as the period as a whole heralds the Canaanite culture that led straight to the Iron Age, every tomb type we know from the Iron Age began in the Middle Bronze Age. Not only are there shaft-and-chamber tombs in the Middle Bronze Age, there are also pit burials under the floors of houses. In-house burial became a regular feature, in big cities and small villages alike. Sometimes the burial pits are not pits at all but elaborately built masonry structures, round and cistlike on occasion, but more often rectangular, the same sort as in later periods.

By the last part of the period, these elaborate tombs become more common within the large cities, a phenomenon that continues into the Late Bronze Age. They are always built of stone, sometimes lined with stones or with bricks, and contain at least two individual inhumations as well as many objects. Even the shaft-and-chamber tombs in outlying cemeteries become larger now, and their offerings more elaborate.

There is a reason for this trend. In the latter half of the Middle Bronze Age, urban life in Canaan is at a high point. It will take the country seven hundred years—until the second half of the Iron Age—before it again reaches this height of development. After several generations of playing "catch-up," the tombs are finally reflecting the wealth and sophistication of the society that made them.

But this does not last. The lag will soon reappear. Burial practices changed so slowly that all through the Late Bronze Age they remained elaborate, in spite of the fact that Canaan had been conquered by a foreign power.

A strange and largely unexplained funerary development of the Middle Bronze Age is the practice of burying equids, generally donkeys, alongside humans. The pits for these graves are extremely large, and the donkeys generally lie on their sides.

Equid burial is a regional phenomenon.[5] The equids are found in sites only in southern Israel as well as in certain tombs in northeast Egypt, tombs that belonged to a group of people known as Hyksos. The Hyksos were a group of Canaanites who had settled in Egypt's delta and who had eventually become rulers in Egypt while retaining their Canaanite identity. The term "Hyksos" is Egyptian for "rulers from foreign lands."

The presence of equids in Hyksos tombs in Egypt suggests that this had become a highly important burial practice. Unfortunately the significance of the buried donkeys is not at all clear. If they were the beasts of burden that belonged to the individuals buried in the tombs, perhaps they were buried to work for the deceased in the afterlife, just as food and drink was left so that the deceased could eat in the afterlife. Or perhaps the donkeys were representative of something else entirely—of power and wealth, and expendable income. They were a purely Canaanite phenomenon, one that ended as suddenly as it began. Equid burials are found only during the Middle Bronze Age, and their presence is still considered largely mysterious.

The Late Bronze Age (1550–1200 B.C.E.)

Like the tombs from the end of the Middle Bronze Age, some of the tombs of Late Bronze Age Canaan are large and sumptuous. Many of them are masonry-constructed, set within the floors of houses within cities, as was the custom.

In the Late Bronze Age tombs of this sort often had tall, corbelled roofs and contained dozens, sometimes hundreds, of pots and objects. Many of these objects were luxury items. Some of them were clearly foreign imports. Some of the corbelled tombs themselves are distinctly Mycenaean in style and are filled with ceramics that were imported from Mycenae.

But this wealth is incongruous, even deceptive, since Canaan was not independent in the Late Bronze Age. Egypt had conquered Canaan and allowed it to exist only as a vassal state. The Egyptians, armed again with a strong central government and army, and angry at the Canaanites (Hyksos) who had briefly ruled their own country, finally struck back. They chased the Hyksos back into Canaan and conquered it in the process. The Egyptian empire ruled Canaan for most of the Late Bronze Age.

But the Egyptians who lived in Canaan were not royalty or even wealthy individuals. They were simply army soldiers sent into a foreign country to keep down rebellions. The fancy tombs of the Late Bronze Age were not made for Egyptian overlords but for private citizens of Canaan.[6]

Possibly the puppet kings of the Canaanite cities were buried in such elaborate structures as a symbolic expression of power. Since they were denied any real power as monarchs while alive, perhaps they took the reins back in death. Still, the many foreign imports and architectural styles of these tombs cannot be dismissed. Another possibility is that these were not the tombs of local kings at all, not even the tombs of local, non-royal citizens. Perhaps these tombs were built for members of an elite class made up in part by foreigners from places as far away as Mycenaean Greece.

Some tombs are certainly of foreigners. A large, corbelled one from Tell Dan, in the northernmost part of Israel, contained a Greek vase that is known as the Charioteer vase because of the depictions on its sides. Forty persons were buried in this tomb—a large number even when several reuses are taken into account. A similar tomb was found at the coastal site of Aphek.

Another tomb, from the site of Gezer, adds credence to this possibility. It contained two Greek larnakes—terra cotta coffins—one with a single inhumation, the other with two persons buried inside. This same tomb contained the scattered remains of ninety other persons, demonstrating a large amount of reuse compared to the Canaanite standard, generally only one or two reuses.

Clearly Greeks, people from the Aegean, were living and dying in Canaan in the Late Bronze Age. These Aegeans must have blended well with the society as a whole, so well that there is little evidence for them besides the contents of these tombs.

Historical evidence for Late Bronze Age Canaan is more abundant than for any other period. A cache of letters found at El-Amarna, Egypt, included hundreds written by Canaanite kings to their Egyptian overlords, asking for help with various situations. In all this literature there is no specific discussion of peoples from the Aegean living in Canaan, or what the role of individual Greeks might have been in the society as a whole.

Because the Amarna letters do not mention Greeks in the land, one can reasonably suppose that these wealthy foreigners did not appear or act significantly different from any other segment of society and did not affect the social, political, or economic landscapes of the country. Here is another instance where burial practices are the last cultural attributes to change. A group of people from far away blended into Canaanite society in every way except in death. In death, they retained their foreignness very clearly.

There were soon to be other new arrivals from the Aegean who did not blend into Canaanite society nearly so well. These people landed on the shores of Canaan at the same time as the Israelites established themselves in the Hill Country, at the very beginning of the Iron Age. The main group of these Aegean peoples went by the name Peleset. They became Israel's arch rival in the Bible. We know them as the Philistines.

The Iron Age (1200 B.C.E.–6TH C B.C.E.)

Minor changes in the burial practices of the Israelites occurred during the long period of the Iron Age, just as they had occurred from period to period. In the eighth century, for instance, we begin to see extremely elaborate shaft-and-chamber burials in the vicinity of Jerusalem, some of them carved with cornices and gabled ceilings. These may well have been the tombs of kings, but like all tombs they are rarely inscribed with names. The idea of blending with one's ancestors for posterity, rather than asserting one's individuality, persisted.

The Israelites borrowed their Cult of the Dead from the Canaanites. The implications of these shared traditions—that these two enemies had more in common than the biblical redactors were comfortable admitting—say worlds about the interaction of the new and the old on the Iron Age landscape. The wild card in the Iron Age deck, the unknown quantity, is the Philistines.

The Philistines hold a unique place in biblical history. They appear throughout the books of Joshua and Judges as well as throughout Kings. The Israelites hated the Philistines perhaps even more than they hated the Canaanites. This hatred has come down to our own time—in modern English, the term "Philistine" describes an uncultured brute, someone we look down on.

The horrendous biblical reputation of the Philistines stems from a number of famous stories as well as some lesser-known ones. Here are the major examples:

> Delilah betrayed Samson by delivering him into the hands of the Philistines. (Judg. 16)
>
> David killed the brutish Goliath, a Philistine, with his slingshot. (1 Sam. 17)
>
> The Philistines killed King Saul and his sons, and hung their decapitated bodies from the walls of their city. (1 Sam. 31)
>
> The Philistines stole the Ark of the Covenant and held it captive in their cities for months. (1 Sam. 4–6)

These and other stories in the Bible describe the strength of the Philistines, the location of their five capital cities on the southern coast of Canaan, and the locations of the Canaanite cities they conquered.

Scholars know a good deal about the Philistines from extra-biblical sources as well, including Egyptian texts and archaeological evidence. The Philistines were not at all philistine; they were a cultivated people, thoughtful artisans and artists, who decorated their pottery with images such as exquisite birds, fish, and spirals.

The Philistines originated in the Aegean, one of several groups known in Egyptian texts as Sea Peoples—people who came in boats from the Aegean to Egypt. At first they fought against the Egyptians, in great battles on land and sea, and then some of them became mercenaries for the Egyptians. The Philistines (as well as some of the other Sea Peoples) lived in Egypt for several generations, fighting in the Egyptian army.

Only after living in Egypt for a while did they move northward, to the southern coastal plain of Canaan.

The Philistines entered Canaan at approximately the same time the Israelites settled the land, at the very end of the Late Bronze Age in the last half of the thirteenth century B.C.E. (The Israelites came into the land at approximately 1200 B.C.E.) The simultaneous entry of these two peoples, each claiming territory that had previously belonged to the Canaanites, explains the deep hatred for the Philistines exhibited in the biblical texts. It was difficult enough for the Israelites, as newcomers, to conquer the land of Canaan, but it was harder still to have to compete with another, stronger group of outsiders.

With the exception of the reign of King Solomon, which is a thin slice of biblical history, the Israelites never ruled the Philistines. In fact, it was not until very late in the history of both groups that the Philistines disappeared archaeologically. The distinctive and beautiful pottery that was a trademark of the Philistines (and that was related to contemporary Aegean styles) continued until the tenth century B.C.E., and Philistine temple architecture and cultic artifacts, also related to Aegean styles, continued to that point as well.

Although the Philistine material record eventually blended with that of the Israelites and Canaanites, they remained a separate political entity for several more centuries, much longer than the Canaanites did. They were still around when Assyria conquered Israel, and they objected to the military campaigns of the Babylonians as fiercely as the Judahites did.

Philistine coffins are one of the several distinctive classes of artifacts that the Philistines left in the archaeological record. Coffins in general were rare in Israel. By the end of the Iron Age they are found in fewer than 10 percent of Israelite tombs. Israelite coffins were made of wood or stone and are sometimes shaped like deep tubs (known as bathtub coffins). Philistine coffins are quite different.

Because the Philistines lived in Egypt as mercenaries for several generations, they began to borrow Egyptian burial practices. This is unusual in and of itself, since burial customs are the last feature that a group ordinarily changes, even when it assimilates. The adoption of native burial practices may mean that the Philistines were actively seeking to be part of Egyptian society.

Philistine coffins were poor man's sarcophagi of the type found in Egypt. In Egypt, members of the middle class who were neither rich nor poor used similar coffins.

In the Late Bronze Age, Egypt ruled Canaan. Archaeologists have found the burials of the Egyptian soldiers stationed at certain sites in Canaan, and these burials contain anthropoid coffins as well. The Egyptian anthropoid coffins are better made than the slightly later Philistine coffins, the features more carefully molded, the attempt to mimic royal sarcophagi very clear.

By the second half of the thirteenth century B.C.E., when their hold on Canaan was already wavering, the Egyptians sent the Philistines into Canaan as mercenaries. At this point in the archaeological record, anthropoid coffins are made by the Philistines themselves, not by the Egyptians. The Philistines who were buried in these coffins did not attempt to pretend they were Egyptian. The molded heads of the coffins portray Philistine feathered headdresses, a type of headdress identifiable on Egyptian reliefs as Philistine. These Philistine mercenaries had blended their own native styles and customs with those of their Egyptian overlords into a new amalgam that suited the new country they lived in.

The Persian and Hellenistic Periods (6th C. B.C.E.–4th C C.E.)

For the small percentage of Judahites who managed to escape the Babylonian exile of 586 B.C.E., life continued without significant material changes. Very few Babylonian customs were imposed on this poorest, least threatening segment of society, people that the Babylonians did not even consider troublesome enough to worry about. When the Persians conquered the land only forty-seven years after the Babylonians had done the same, Iron Age burial practices segued into Persian period ones undisturbed.

But by the Hellenistic period in Palestine, the physical landscape of ancient Israel had changed considerably, with huge amphitheaters, aqueducts, and palaces eventually covering the ground. Tombs, however, changed only slightly from their Iron Age forms. The more interesting change in this period is the philosophical change in the approach to death. Rabbinic Judaism had now been born, and rabbinic academies flourished in Palestine as the rabbis composed the Oral Law (the Talmud).

Coffins

During the biblical period, coffins were rarely used in ancient Israel. The Philistines and Egyptians who lived in Canaan would sometimes use them, and there is archaeological evidence for an occasional wooden or stone coffin from the Iron Age.

But coffins did not come into common use until the Roman period. Jesus, who died in about 30 C.E., was not placed in a coffin but was rather carried on a bier (Mark 16.1; Luke 23.5–6, 7.11–17; John 19.40), but Rabbi Yohanan ben Zakkai was carried out of Jerusalem in a coffin in 70 C.E.

A rabbinic anecdote surrounding Rabbi Yohanan ben Zakkai's coffin makes it clear that coffins came into common use between 30 and 70 C.E. The anecdote involves the moving of the Great Assembly, the Jewish legislative body, out of Jerusalem following the 70 C.E. Roman destruction. According to the anecdote, Rabbi Yohanan, who then headed the Great Assembly, sneaked out of Jerusalem. His men placed him in a coffin alive and carried him out of the city. This was the perfect means of escape, because while the Romans allowed no one to leave Jerusalem during the time of their siege, they did permit the removal of the dead for burial outside the city. After Rabbi Yohanan had escaped the city in this manner, he managed to reconvene the Great Assembly in the quiet town of Yavneh, with the permission of the Roman emperor.

Although possibly fictional, this anecdote establishes that coffins were commonly used by Jews in Palestine in the Roman period. The Roman soldiers guarding Jerusalem did not give Rabbi Yohanan's coffin a second thought.

Although coffins were commonplace in the country by the middle of the first century C.E., they never completely pushed out the tradition of coffinless burial, which remains the most common type of burial in the Middle East today. The explanation for this comes from a line in the Bible:

> For out of it [the ground] you were taken; you are dust, and to dust you shall return. (Gen. 3.19)

The idea that man is made of dust or clay and must be returned to dust is implicit in the tradition of coffinless burial, as coffins only hinder the decomposition process by which the body returns to dust.

When coffins are used (both in the Middle East and elsewhere), Jewish tradition dictates that they be made only of plain pine. This ruling goes back to the second century C.E., when Rabbi Gamliel II, then head of the Great Assembly, announced that he wished his burial to take place in a plain coffin, as a response to most of the other coffins of the day. Coffins had become so elaborate and expensive that Rabbi Gamliel criticized them, saying that such coffins placed material wealth above spiritual purity.

Since Rabbi Gamliel II, Jews who use coffins use only simple ones. This custom also served as a way for the Jews to differentiate themselves from the Christians, as Christians of the day used elaborate coffins. Judaism and Christianity were already severely at odds with each other, and Rabbi Gamliel himself had added a curse against Christians to the Jewish daily prayer service. Restricting the types of coffins that Jews used was one way for the Jews to separate themselves from the early Christians.

Ossuaries

Besides the use of coffins, one of the most interesting mortuary developments of the Hellenistic period is the ossuary burial. Ossuaries had been used only once before in Israel, in the Chalcolithic period, but these burial practices did not continue.

Ossuaries appear again in the first century C.E., and their decorations and inscriptions are indicative of the people who made them. Because of the injunction in the Bible against forming images of God, and because the Bible also states that man was created in God's image, a rabbinic tradition developed prohibiting, or at least restricting, artistic images of men as well as images of God. Ossuaries were therefore never decorated with human images but with floral ones.

A small class of ossuaries shows architectural decoration. One ossuary, from the first century B.C.E., is made to look like masonry work, both on the sides and on the roof. Another, also from the first century, is extremely elaborate, with doors, complete with triangular lintels, columns, and windows with rounded tops.

The striking feature of these architectural ossuaries is the similarity of their designs to those of Chalcolithic ossuaries. Both periods show that there were attempts to make bone repositories into houses. While there is no stylistic comparison (Chalcolithic ossuaries are deeply rooted in the artistic tradition of that period), the motivation is the same. Here, in the clearest possible way, ossuaries are made into houses. The families of the dead had the same motivation throughout the centuries, from the Chalcolithic period to the Bronze Age to the Iron Age, always seeking to give their dead family members a proper place to live.

First-century ossuaries are box shaped, approximately two feet long by one foot wide and one foot deep. They are generally made of the ubiquitous white limestone found in most of Israel. Most ossuaries have decorative carvings, some have simple inscriptions—phrases such as "Father," "Mother," "Do not open," or "These are the bones of . . ."

Rosettes are one of the most common decorative motifs for ossuaries. Many ossuaries have an exquisitely carved and complex rosette on each of the longer sides. They also generally have borders, often running spirals, along both their top and bottom edges.[7]

Once an ossuary was filled and sealed, it was placed in a tomb. The most common tombs were acrosolia, the late Iron Age derivation of Bronze Age shaft-and-chamber tombs. Acrosolia are always square or rectangular in shape, consisting of a squarish chamber from which narrow rectangular slots, or chambers, project, each large enough to house a single person. Like their Bronze Age predecessors, acrosolia were likely used for groupings of nuclear or extended families.[8]

There is little evidence about the place of primary interment for those corpses whose bones were later placed in ossuaries. The most likely possibility is that the bodies may have been allowed to decay within the tombs themselves. When the appropriate amount of time had passed, the family members would reenter the tomb with an ossuary, collect all the bones that they could fit into the ossuary, then leave the ossuary in the same tomb.

It is not known whether a second funeral was conducted with the secondary burial in an ossuary. Rabbinic texts are completely and mysteriously silent on this point, in spite of the fact that ossuaries are commonly found in first-century Judean tombs. Nor do any other written sources mention any such ceremony.

Perhaps secondary burial was so well accepted within the society that no mentions of it were necessary. Or ossuary burial may have been a folk custom that never was officially sanctioned and therefore never was mentioned in the literature of the official religion of the period. These two possibilities are not exclusive of each other. Ossuary burial may have been both extremely common as well as unsanctioned.

Jewish ossuaries have brought us almost full circle. Although there is no known connection between these ossuaries and their Chalcolithic predecessors, the form remained—or rather reappeared—in the exact same locale, attesting to the persistence of ideas related to death and afterlife.

This persistence of burial and tomb form from period to period is extraordinary, especially considering how different the cultures of the earlier parts of the Bronze Age were from those of the later parts of the Iron Age. Within the land of ancient Israel, little to no change in death practices was the rule.

But what about the neighbors of ancient Israel? Did they

share the Israelites' beliefs about death and afterlife? The Bible discusses the peoples of Egypt and Mesopotamia in depth. Did the death practices of these well-known neighbors, neighbors who left extensive written records, affect the Israelite Cult of the Dead, or vice versa?

4

The Death Customs and Beliefs of Israel's Neighbors

Burial practices are very slow to change. The Canaanite Cult of the Dead persisted in the face of monotheism, and ancient tomb shapes and types of tomb offerings continued for millennia with few interruptions.

Israelite death practices not only bridged mountain ranges and deserts, connecting ancient Israel to all its neighbors, they also bridged languages and various gods and religions. People in Mesopotamia and Syria, as well as in Egypt, all practiced ancestor cults that were remarkably similar to that of the Israelites.

This in and of itself should not be too surprising, as both the Bible and nonbiblical texts tell us that these cultures interacted economically and politically. What is surprising, coming from the nonliterate world of ancient Israel, is that these neighboring cultures wrote down their beliefs about death and afterlife and even recorded portions of their death rituals. There are no written sources for death practices in ancient Israel except the Bible itself, but we have texts from Mesopotamia and Syria that tell exactly what was going on in those countries concerning death.

For mortuary studies, these foreign texts are as exciting as missing links. Because these cultures have archaeological records that connect them to the world of ancient Israel, and because, for instance, the Syrians and the Mesopotamians buried their dead under the floors of houses just as the Israelites did, the Syrians and Mesopotamians should also have attitudes toward death similar to those of the Israelites.

The written texts from these neighboring lands provide exactly the information lacking from Israel, information regarding attitudes toward death and burial. This adds significantly to our knowledge of death in the biblical world.

The Bible not only admits, it proclaims that its cultural origins are in Mesopotamia. The two worlds, one monotheistic and a fringe culture, the other polytheistic and a major, influential cultural center, clearly have a common origin. Stated more precisely, the main origins of biblical culture, including biblical perceptions of death and afterlife, lie in Mesopotamian religion and folklore.

The Bible describes the Garden of Eden as the source of four rivers, two of which are the Tigris and the Euphrates, the two main rivers of Mesopotamia (Gen. 2.10–14). This biblical geography situates the Garden of Eden in Mesopotamia proper. Similarly, the biblical flood story has an exact Mesopotamian parallel. And, most strikingly, Abraham, the first biblical patriarch, was born in Ur, one of Mesopotamia's main cities. With these deep, self-proclaimed connections, it is only natural to look to Mesopotamian death mythologies for parallels with biblical attitudes toward death.

Mesopotamian and Biblical Perceptions of Death

One of the few well-known pieces of Mesopotamian literature is the *Epic of Gilgamesh.* The reason this ancient epic holds general and not just scholarly interest is that it contains a flood story very similar to the one in the Bible.[1] This has fascinated professional and lay people alike since it was first discovered more than a hundred years ago.

But the Mesopotamian flood story is only the tail end of the *Epic of Gilgamesh,* a long and complex text. The main theme of this Mesopotamian epic is the quest for immortality and the inevitability of death. The Mesopotamians and the biblical Israelites shared a great fear of death. Both groups also harbored a fruitless hope for immortality. These two death-related themes are integral to the *Epic of Gilgamesh.*

The first half of the *Epic of Gilgamesh* concerns the deep friendship between Gilgamesh, king of Uruk, and Enkidu, his alter ego. Gilgamesh and Enkidu engage in all sorts of exploits. They walk miles together just to kill a monster in a faraway forest. They come home and tease goddesses. Eventually they go too far. They throw the great Bull of Heaven at the goddess Ishtar, who is enraged. Ishtar wants to punish them. As punishment, Enkidu becomes sick and dies.

The second part of the story concerns Gilgamesh's reaction

to Enkidu's death. He mourns for his friend inconsolably, and his grief starts him on a far-reaching quest for immortality.

Toward the end of the story, Gilgamesh locates a man said to be immortal, named Utnapishtim.[2] Utnapishtim reluctantly tells Gilgamesh how to gain immortality: There is a plant that grows on the bottom of the sea. If Gilgamesh can get that plant and eat it, he too will become immortal.

Gilgamesh goes to the sea, puts weights on his legs in order to sink to the bottom, plucks the plant, and rises back to the surface. But he does not eat the plant immediately. Wanting to clean himself after his long quest, he sees a well and bathes in it. As he bathes, a snake comes by, steals the plant of immortality, and presumably eats it. Man loses his immortality.

The parallels to Genesis 3—the story of Adam and Eve and the serpent—fairly jump off the page. In Genesis 3, a serpent encourages Eve to eat fruit from the forbidden Tree of Knowledge, the one tree that God declared off-limits. Eve eats, then encourages Adam to eat as well. When God punishes Adam and Eve for this disobedience, he sentences them to ultimate death:

> In the sweat of your face you shall eat bread till you return to the ground, for out of it you were taken; you are dust, and to dust you shall return. (Gen. 3.19)

Returning to dust—that is, dying—is a result of listening to the serpent. As in the Gilgamesh *Epic*, a snake causes mankind to lose his chance at immortality. In Genesis the snake acts by persuasion, and in Gilgamesh by stealing the plant of immortality for himself.

These stories were related in the distant past of both cultures. The biblical redactors took a Mesopotamian theme—serpents and the loss of immortality—and combined it with one of their own: punishment for not obeying God.

In the biblical story, eating food caused Adam to lose immortality; in the Mesopotamian version, eating food would have given Gilgamesh immortality.

Other Mesopotamian myths also contain this biblical association between food and immortality. One myth concerns a man named Adapa, who cursed the south wind for tipping over his fishing boat. The god Anu is furious at him for daring to curse the south wind and demands that he appear before him. Adapa's own god, Ea, gives him advice before he goes for his audience. Do not eat or drink anything that Anu offers you, Ea tells him, because it will be the food and drink of death.

When Anu offers Adapa food and drink during their meeting, he remembers the warning and does not eat. But it turns out that Anu has tricked him—it wasn't the food and drink of death he offered, but of life, of immortality. Had Adapa not listened so well to Ea's warnings, he could have become immortal.

As in Genesis and the Gilgamesh *Epic,* food can both bestow and remove immortality. Adapa lost immortality because he listened too closely to the words of a god and did not eat when he should have. Similarly, Adam lost immortality because he did not listen closely enough to the words of God and ate when he should not have. But here is where the biblical redactors changed a small but significant detail: In the Mesopotamian case, blind obedience to the divine is not good, while in the biblical tale, blind obedience to the divine is extremely important.

Even though the religious messages are different, the themes of the stories—food, obedience, immortality—are the same. The belief about immortality in the two cultures was also the same, as was the fear of death. In both cultures, as much as man wishes to be immortal—and godlike in immortality—he cannot. He will ultimately die.

The Mesopotamian and Biblical Netherworlds

In another story from the Gilgamesh cycle (although not from the *Epic* itself), Enkidu talks to Gilgamesh after he is already dead, describing the Netherworld to him in terrifying terms.

The Netherworld is a place of horrors—it is filthy, and vermin crawl all over its inhabitants. In response to a question from Gilgamesh, Enkidu reports that all the dead have the same fate in the Netherworld—there are no divisions between people of rank and commoners. Kings such as Gilgamesh will be like everyone else in death. The Netherworld, while a place of horrors, is egalitarian.

The egalitarianism is echoed in the Bible in a passage of Isaiah: "[The king of Babylon is] brought down to She'ol, to the depths of the pit" (Isa. 14.15). Death was the great equalizer, even in the biblical world. It could lower even the king of Babylon himself to the same level as all the other dead who reside in the pit of She'ol, the biblical term for the Netherworld.[3]

The Mesopotamian Netherworld is more vividly described

than the biblical one. Besides Enkidu's description, a text exists from the seventh century B.C.E. about a man named Kumma who was granted a vision of the Netherworld. Kumma sees frightening images, including a serpent-headed man, a lion-headed man with two sets of arms and legs, and an ox-headed man, also with two sets of arms and legs. He describes Nergal, one of the rulers of the Netherworld, with lightning flashing from his arms.

In spite of the vividness of the nonbiblical descriptions, the salient features of the biblical and Mesopotamian netherworlds are alike. Not only do they both level the dead from all walks of life, they are physically similar to each other. Both places are beneath the earth, both have roads leading to them, and both have gates at their entrances.

Here is a description of the Mesopotamian netherworld:

> Ishtar set [out] to the Land of No Return. . . . To the road from which there is no way back. . . . Where dust is their [the inhabitants] fare and clay their food, [where] they see no light, residing in darkness . . . where over door and bolt is spread dust . . . Ishtar reached the gate of No Return. She said these words to the gatekeeper. "O gatekeeper, open thy gate . . ." (From the Descent of Ishtar to the Netherworld, lines 1–13)[4]

Similarly, biblical descriptions of She'ol include the following:

> Thy dead . . . O dwellers in the dust . . . (Isa. 26.19)

> Will [my hope] go down to the bars of She'ol? Shall we descend together into the dust? (Job 17.16)

> The waves of death encompassed me, the torrents of perdition assailed me; the cords of She'ol entangled me, the snares of death confronted me. (2 Sam. 22.5–6, and nearly identical text in Ps. 18.5–6)

> I shall go down to She'ol . . . (Gen. 37.35)

These quotes parallel the Mesopotamian ones regarding the dead living in dust in the Netherworld, and also echo some of the horrors of the Netherworld seen in the Mesopotamian text. The latter quotes establish the physicality of She'ol as a place below ground (cf. Gen. 37.5), often called a pit (cf. Isa. 14.15), both descriptions common to the Mesopotamian Netherworld. And just as the Mesopotamian Netherworld had locked gates, She'ol is likened to a prison, with bars to block entry and exit (cf. Job. 17.16).

Other passages in the Bible refer to She'ol as a place where God's presence does not extend. God does not remember the dead in She'ol, nor are the dead able to remember or praise God there. The root of the word She'ol itself means hollowness.

> For She'ol cannot thank thee [God], death cannot praise thee; those who go down to the Pit cannot hope for thy faithfulness. (Isa. 38.18)

> For in death there is no remembrance of thee [God]; in She'ol who can give thee praise? (Ps. 6.5)

> I am reckoned among those who go down to the Pit . . . like one forsaken among the dead, like the slain that lie in the grave, like those whom thou dost remember no more, for they are cut off from thy hand. (Ps. 88.4–5)

Based on these descriptions of She'ol, people not only feared the idea of death but also the place itself. For a people who had only one God, the idea of being in an underground prison outside of that God's jurisdiction was devastating.

But if God had no place in She'ol, who did? In Mesopotamia there was a goddess of the Netherworld named Ereshkigal. The Netherworld was her domain, and no other gods were allowed there. Was there a comparable ruler of She'ol?

Gods and Goddesses of Death

Ereshkigal, queen of the Mesopotamian underworld, is definitely not a devil-like character, nor does she embody evil. Instead, Ereshkigal is somewhat sympathetic, even lovable.[5]

In one myth, Ereshkigal falls in love with another deity, Nergal. Nergal is a reluctant lover at first, disguising himself in order to avoid Ereshkigal, but every time he sees her, he finds her irresistible and falls in love all over again. Eventually Nergal becomes Ereshkigal's permanent consort, ruling the Netherworld alongside her.

Ereshkigal is clearly depicted as sympathetic in this story. In one version she even cries. Although she certainly can be ruthless (when she gets angry at Nergal she wants to kill him), overall she is not only sympathetic but even pathetic—a woman scorned. In this story it is almost as if her role as queen of the Netherworld is irrelevant—it is just a job, one that sometimes gets in the way of who she really wants to be.

Even when her role as mistress of the Netherworld is the

main point of a myth, Ereshkigal is still sympathetic, or at the very least understandable. In the myth called "Ishtar's Descent to the Underworld," Ishtar, goddess of love, wishes to descend to the Netherworld to pay her respects to Ereshkigal.[6] When Ishtar finally passes through the gates of the Netherworld and into Ereshkigal's throne room, she dies. Her servant goes for help. Eventually Ishtar is sprinkled with the Water of Life, and revives.

The story ends with a bargain. Ereshkigal allows Ishtar to leave the Netherworld, but only if she sends back a replacement for herself. Ishtar chooses her brother Dumuzi as the replacement. Dumuzi must split the year with his sister, each living in the Netherworld for six months.[7]

If Ereshkigal were an evil queen of the Netherworld, she would never let the goddess of love leave her domain. But Ereshkigal is not a caricature of evil. She acts humanly, like any of the other deities in the pantheon.

If She'ol had a ruler, what was he like? Was he sympathetic and lovable, like Ereshkigal?

There were other underworld deities in the Mesopotamian and Syrian worlds, and not all of them were as sympathetic as Ereshkigal. One of these was Motu, underworld deity of the Ugaritic world.

Ugarit is a loose term for northern, coastal Canaan, the same region known as Phoenicia in the Iron Age. We have seen how the Israelite Cult of the Dead was really an extension of the Canaanite Cult of the Dead, a cult that pervaded all of Canaanite territory, north and south. Death beliefs in the mythology of Ugarit include a voracious, man-eating god named Motu. The Canaanite god of death, Motu was known for many millennia over a large geographic area. Vestiges of him can be found in the Hebrew Bible itself.

Motu is not a sympathetic god. He lives in a pit of mud and acts like a monster, chewing up and swallowing humans in a single bite.

> Approach not Divine Mot, lest he make you like a lamb in his mouth. Ye be crushed like a kid in his gullet. (Ba'al and Anat Poems, e.II AB viii, lines 18–20)

In one story about Motu, he eats Ba'al, the chief Canaanite god. Ba'al's lover Anat is furious at Motu and takes revenge by killing him—killing death itself. But after seven years, Motu is alive again and agrees to release Ba'al if he receives a substitute instead. The story ends with the substitution of Motu's own brother for Ba'al.

This story clearly parallels Mesopotamian Ereshkigal's release of Ishtar, and Ishtar's substitution of her brother for herself. Canaanite mythologies and thoughts about the Netherworld were not far removed from those of Mesopotamia.

Israelite Deities of Death

And Israelite beliefs were not far removed from Canaanite beliefs, even though a surface reading of the biblical passages relating to She'ol reveals no ruler at all, much less one like Motu.

But a closer reading of the biblical texts, and the vocabulary of death that they use, shows a very different reality. The Hebrew word for "dead" is "Met." The past tense of the verb "to die," is "Mot." "Death," a grammatical variant of the same root, is "Mavet," also read "Mot."[8]

The Hebrew word for death is actually the name of the Canaanite god of death himself. While this is not entirely surprising—Ugaritic and Hebrew are both Semitic languages and as such share word roots—it is not just grammatical happenstance either. The Hebrew term "Mot" reflects the evolution of Israelite religion.

The Israelites lived among Canaanites, and in the distant past they may have shared a religion. We see that not merely in the persistence of the Cult of the Dead but also in this vestige of a term. Sometime in the distant past the very She'ol that the Israelites feared was ruled by the god Mot.

A similar linguistic vestige of polytheism has to do with a north Syrian goddess named Shuwala. Shuwala is a goddess of death mentioned in texts from a city called Emar, along the Euphrates River. These ritual texts clearly identify Shuwala as the Syrian variant of Ereshkigal, Mesopotamian queen of the Netherworld.

Shuwala is cognate with She'ol—the underworld of the Hebrew Bible. In fact, She'ol is a feminine noun in Hebrew, most likely reflecting its origins as a name of a female goddess. The goddess of death has become the place she rules, She'ol.

It is even possible to conjecture that Shuwala and Motu were still active gods in biblical Israel. In certain biblical passages these terms almost certainly represent more than just metaphors of poetic language. In Isaiah 28, people who scoff at God say,

> "We have made a covenant with Death [Mavet/Mot] and with She'ol we have made an agreement." (Isa. 28.15)

And later in the same chapter,

> And [God] will make justice the line, and righteousness the plummet. . . . Then your covenant with Death [Mavet/Mot] will be annulled, and your agreement with She'ol will not stand . . . (Isa. 28.17–19)

In these references, Mavet and She'ol may well be actual personages, deities with whom one can collaborate.

The biblical redactors could not remove every vestige of polytheism, especially not when it came to death; there were too many. The biblical Netherworld was ruled by at least one god and possibly by a goddess as well, monotheism notwithstanding.

The Evidence from Egypt

Mesopotamian texts reveal that Mesopotamian attitudes toward death and its inevitability were similar to biblical attitudes, that Mesopotamian peoples shared the unrealized biblical quest for immortality, and that the two places had very similar underworlds ruled by comparable deities.

Death in Egypt, on the other hand, looks quite different. Egypt, Israel's other powerful neighbor, is the setting for many of the formative stories of the Bible, including the Joseph stories.

Egyptian religion was largely death-centered. Each Egyptian king spent his entire life constructing a pyramid under which he would be buried. The massive pyramid-tombs were filled with enormous riches. Because the body was essential in the afterlife, the Egyptians had themselves embalmed for preservation.

Egyptian priests would read numerous prayers and incantations to help the dead person get to the afterlife. The mortuary cults of the greatest Egyptian kings were maintained for centuries after their deaths. In short, everything the Egyptians did concerning death was on a large scale, the antithesis of the small-scale practices of neighboring Canaan.

In spite of vast cultural differences, the literature of Egypt offers small, neglected tidbits concerning the burial practices of the Canaanites and Israelites. The Egyptians themselves noticed the differences between their own death practices and those of their neighbors. A famous Egyptian tale known as the "Story of Sinuhe" includes the only extra-biblical description of a Canaanite/Israelite funeral and burial.

Sinuhe, an Egyptian royal steward, overhears the details of a plot to kill the king. Afraid of being implicated, he runs away, as far north as he can, to escape the reach of the Egyptians. He finally stops somewhere along the Syrian coast. Once there he settles down, and a local sheik takes him under his wing. He marries the sheik's daughter and begins a tribe of his own.

Even though Sinuhe describes his adopted land of Canaan in loving terms, toward the end of his life he reestablishes ties with Egypt. The Egyptian king (the son of the one murdered in the plot) invites him to return to Egypt, since it would be terrible for an Egyptian to die and be buried outside of Egypt.

At this point in the narrative, the fantastic Egyptian funeral ceremony is contrasted with the extremely simple Canaanite one. This description, brief and biased as it is, is the only one we have of a Canaanite funeral.

> It should not be that thou shouldst die in a foreign country. Asiatics should not escort thee. Thou shouldst not be placed in a sheepskin when thy wall is made. This is too long to be roaming the earth. (Story of Sinuhe, lines 195 ff.)

This passage reveals that Canaanite burials had a procession. "Asiatics should not escort thee" refers to a procession in which the body was escorted by natives of the land, presumably family members. While a funeral procession is not surprising, this is the only reference to one in an ancient text referring to Canaan.

The next sentence is even more exciting. "When thy wall is made" corroborates the archaeological evidence for a specific type of tomb. The term "wall" refers to the tomb itself, and cannot mean the simple pit tombs but rather one of the more elaborate architectural types. Canaanite and Israelite masonry tombs were similar to Egyptian tombs in that both used stone as part of the structure.

Lastly, the line "Thou shouldst not be placed in a sheepskin" teaches something else entirely new about Canaanite burial practices: the body was wrapped in a shroud made of sheepskin. This is the only reference to a shroud of any sort. The use of sheepskin implies that a sheep was killed, probably sacrificed as part of the funerary rituals, and also implies that sheepskin shrouds might not have been used at all funerals, as a certain amount of wealth was necessary in order to have a sheep disposable for such a purpose.[9]

This reference to sheepskin shrouds is unique. The Sinuhe text is therefore an extremely important extra-biblical source for the funerary practices of the Canaanites.

The Deaths of Jacob and Joseph

The Egyptians believed that every person had to be preserved individually, because everyone needed his own body intact in the afterlife. This was why Sinuhe thought it was so important to be buried in Egypt—burial in Canaan would not ensure his survival into the afterlife.

Individual preservation for the afterlife was completely at odds with the beliefs of the Canaanites and Israelites, who were happy to be buried in their ancestral tombs, their bones mixing with the bones of their fathers. The Sinuhe story shows that Egyptians were horrified by this mixing.

These differing philosophies explain why Canaanite and Egyptian funerary practices were so different. But in that case, two deaths in the Bible are problematical. Why were Jacob and his son Joseph—two of the most important ancestors of the Israelites—not only buried in an Egyptian manner but mummified as well?

The fact that Jacob and Joseph died in Egypt is not enough

of a rationale. The passages concerning their burials are extremely specific.

> Then [Jacob] charged [his sons], and said to them, "I am to be gathered to my people; bury me with my fathers in the cave that is in the field of Ephron the Hittite, in the cave that is in the field at Machpelah, to the east of Mamre, in the land of Canaan, which Abraham bought with the field from Ephron the Hittite to possess as a burying place. There they buried Abraham and Sarah his wife; there they buried Isaac and Rebekah his wife; and there I buried Leah—the field and the cave that is in it were purchased from the Hittites. (Gen. 49.29–32)

The details of the description are not gratuitous; on the contrary, they serve as a map with several intentionally redundant landmarks—the field that was bought from Ephron the Hittite, at Machpelah, east of Mamre. The redundancies were to ensure that Jacob's children, who may never have been to the family burial plot, would find it no matter what. Even though Jacob chose to live in Egypt, being with his ancestors after death was more important than where he resided during life.

Of course, carrying a body from Egypt to Canaan would take days if not weeks, and the climate was hot. Jacob himself made no specific wish to be embalmed in the Egyptian manner, especially since he wished his bones to be mixed into the tomb of his ancestors, but mummification was the only way his body could be transported back to Canaan. Joseph, therefore, had him mummified:

> And Joseph commanded his servants the physicians to embalm his father. So the physicians embalmed [Jacob]; forty days were required for it, for so many are required for embalming. And the Egyptians wept for him seventy days. (Gen. 50.2–3)

> And when the days of weeping for him were past, . . . [Jacob's] sons did for him as he had commanded them; for his sons carried him to the land of Canaan and buried him in the cave of the field at Machpelah. . . . After he had buried his father, Joseph returned to Egypt with his brothers and all who had gone up with him to bury his father. (Gen. 50.4–14)

The time frames given in the first passage are not in accord with lengths of mourning specified in the Bible, but they are in exact agreement with what is known about Egyptian embalming.[10]

During the process of embalming, the embalmers removed all the organs and bodily fluids from the body, then packed it in natron, a saltlike chemical, to dry out. After the body was sufficiently dry, the embalmers soaked linens in fragrant spices and placed them inside the body cavities, and rubbed resins on the skin. Finally they bandaged the body in linen strips, wrapping amulets and jewelry in between the strips.

The entire embalming process took seventy days, exactly the time that the Egyptians mourned Jacob. But the most important part of the embalming process was the time the body spent drying out in the natron. The natron soak took forty days, the time specified for embalming in the biblical passage quoted above. The Egyptians mourned Jacob from the moment he died until his mummy was complete, as they would mourn any Egyptian, because Jacob's mortuary treatment was completely Egyptian.

The biblical passages show that mummification was not prohibited by Israelite custom, at least not in this early period. When Joseph dies, he too is mummified, for the same reasons.

Like his father, Joseph asks for burial in Canaan, though not specifically in the tomb at Machpelah (he is buried at Shechem). Like Jacob, Joseph's body must be mummified for transport to Canaan, especially since he is not brought to Canaan immediately but waits in Egypt for several hundred years, until Moses brings the Israelites back to Canaan:

> So Joseph dwelt in Egypt. . . . And Joseph said to his brothers, "I am about to die; but God will visit you, and bring you up out of this land to the land which he swore to Abraham, to Isaac and to Jacob. . . . God will visit you, and you shall carry my bones from here." So Joseph died . . . and he was put in a coffin in Egypt. (Gen. 50.22–26)

> And the people of Israel went up out of the land of Egypt equipped for battle. And Moses took the bones of Joseph with him; for Joseph had solemnly sworn . . . saying "God will visit you; then you must carry my bones with you from here." (Exod. 14.18–19)

> The bones of Joseph which the people of Israel brought up from Egypt were buried at Shechem, in the portion of

> ground which Jacob brought from the sons of Hamor the father of Shechem for a hundred pieces of money; it became an inheritance of the descendants of Joseph. (Josh. 24.32)

The end of the first passage, "and he was put in a coffin in Egypt," implies that Joseph was mummified immediately after his death, though the term itself is not used. The other passages, which describe how the Israelites carried his "bones" with them to Canaan and buried them there, confirm that these are mummified remains preserved well enough to survive intact for generations.

Whatever the differences in beliefs about the afterlife between the Israelites and the Egyptians, burial place was extremely important to both groups. The Story of Sinuhe discussed above shows that it was imperative for an Egyptian to die in Egypt so that he could receive proper Egyptian burial treatment.

The biblical stories demonstrate the same objective—that the ancestors of the Israelites wished to be buried in the Land of Israel above all else, even if it meant receiving an Egyptian burial treatment. Their desire to be buried in their own land, itself a reassertion of the biblical claim on the Land of Israel, and their desire to be buried with their ancestors in that land, were more important than any other aspects of their death beliefs and practices.

But what happened to the biblical and Mesopotamian beliefs about death, the Netherworld, and afterlife when the biblical period came to an end? And what happened to the biblical

She'ol—how did it transform itself from a physical, prisonlike place to the Judeo-Christian idea of heaven and hell? This transformation involved the addition of new ideas, rather than the loss of old ones. Nothing about death was ever lost. Old ideologies were simply transformed according to the cultural norms of later times.

5

The Biblical Origins of Hell and the Devil

After the Babylonians conquered Judah in 586 B.C.E., they sent the Judahites up to Babylon to live in exile. This exile, and the subsequent existence as a Diaspora religion, transformed ancient Israelite religion into Judaism. The Jews (as they came to be known) were now distant from the world of the Bible in terms of both time and place. In Babylon they were forced to interact with other Near Eastern and then Western peoples. First they lived among the Babylonians, then the Persians, then the Greeks, and finally the Romans.

This progression of overlords significantly affected the death beliefs and practices of the Jews. At first the changes in ritual that developed during these periods were only minor. Not until later, in the Talmudic period, did more important additions occur. Through it all though, biblical ideas remained a backdrop to the death practices.

The changes in death-related beliefs, as opposed to rituals, also began as minor ones—simple thoughts that helped the Jewish community rationalize its exilic existence. They were no longer living in the Land of Israel, and their religion had to accommodate this fact, not only in terms of the loss of the Temple but also in terms of death rites.

As the Jews' memories of their aboriginal Canaanite polytheism faded into the distant past, the idea of underworld deities such as Motu and Shuwala faded as well. In the absence of underworld deities, post-Exilic Jews were forced to postulate a single God who created both good and evil, and who controlled both good and evil impulses. Such a god was difficult to imagine, which is why some of the early rabbis dared to change the words of the Bible in the liturgical texts that they wrote. They changed the text so that God was no longer responsible for creating evil.

An original biblical quotation is as follows:

> I form light and create darkness, I make peace and create evil. (Isa. 45.7)

But in the daily prayer service that the early rabbis put together, this quote is changed to:

> Praised be You, O Lord our God, King of the universe, Who forms light and creates darkness, Who makes peace and creates all things.

According to early Jewish philosophy, God cannot be the creator of evil—it is too difficult to imagine, therefore the term "evil" is removed, subsumed under a more general category of "all things."[1]

With this as a premise, it is not surprising that the Exilic communities took on the idea of an anti-God, a devil, along with a concept of hell as a substitute for the ancient underworld. Some of this was a development of Exilic Judaism, and some of it—the devil part—was a development of early Christianity, which in turn influenced the Jewish beliefs of a slightly later period.

The Origins of Hell

She'ol, a typical Near Eastern underworld, evolved into the modern Judeo-Christian hell, complete with fire and brimstone and a fork-tailed devil, through the combination of several unrelated traditions.

The first of these was a Canaanite tradition. According to the Bible, the Canaanites had a custom of sacrificing children to a god called Moloch. While there is no archaeological evidence for Canaanite child sacrifice in ancient Israel, something like it may have occasionally been practiced by groups of Canaanites elsewhere.[2]

Whatever the practice amounted to in reality, the Israelites were horrified by the concept of child sacrifice and repeatedly referred to this purported custom when they needed anti-Canaanite propaganda (see for instance 2 Kings 23.10). What could make a people appear worse than sacrificing their own children? After all, Abraham, the forefather of the Israelites, had *almost* sacrificed his son to Yahweh, but Yahweh had stopped him at the last minute. The Israelite God would never allow child sacrifice, and the fact that the Canaanite gods courted it made them reprehensible in the eyes of the Israelites.

According to this anti-Canaanite propaganda, the Canaanites performed these sacrifices to Moloch at a place called Tophet, located in a particular valley known as Geh ben Hinnom, the "Valley of Hinnom's Son," sometimes translated as the "Valley of the Screaming Son," a translation that may derive from the practice itself. "Geh ben Hinnom" was sometimes abbreviated as just "Geh Hinnom" (see for instance Josh. 18.6).

"Geh Hinnom" devolved in the Rabbinic period into "Gehenna," which is the only, rather inexact, Jewish term for hell.[3] Nothing, after all, is more hellish than sacrificing one's own children. Somewhere between the biblical world and the later Rabbinic period, Gehenna replaced She'ol as the hellish home of the dead.

Another, even more significant, set of traditions that allowed the Jewish concept of hell to evolve was Persian. The Jews lived under Persian rule from the late sixth century B.C.E. until the fourth century B.C.E., when the Greeks conquered the East. The Persians, an Iranian people, had several capital cities in the southwestern part of Iran, not far from the border with Babylonia. The Persians were initially benevolent overlords, allowing any Jew who wished to return from exile in Babylon to do so. Some Jews did in fact return to Jerusalem (where they built the Second Temple with Persian permission), while others moved to Persia itself (as the story of the Jewish holiday Purim attests), and still others remained in what had been Babylon.

Because of their constant contact with Persian culture and religion, the Jews integrated various aspects of Persian culture into their own culture and religion, as they had done with Babylonian culture, and as they would do with the cultures of many future ruling cultures, including those of the Greeks and Romans. The aspect of Persian culture that was most easily integrated was a main one that fully permeated the Persian mindset. This was the concept of duality.

Zoroastrianism, the religion of the ancient Persians, is still practiced today in parts of India and Iran. Zoroaster, also known as Zarathrustra, was the original prophet of Zoroastrianism. It is unclear when Zoroaster lived, but the Persians were already Zoroastrians in the sixth century B.C.E.

The major benevolent god of Zoroastrianism is Ahura Mazda, a god of light.[4] Ahura Mazda's evil opposite is Angra Mainyu, the "Lord of Lies," who symbolizes darkness and death. This duality of light/good, darkness/evil permeated the religion. According to Zoroastrian beliefs, the duality will come to a head in a final cosmic battle between good and evil, in which the soul of man will hang in the balance. In the end, evil will be vanquished, hell will be destroyed, the dead will be resurrected, and the kingdom of heaven on earth will begin.

In Zoroastrianism, the soul is judged after death. If the outcome is good, the soul is brought to the House of Song. If it is bad, the soul descends to hell, which is not ruled by Angra Mainyu but by the first man ever to die.

This good/evil duality came to permeate Judaism during the Persian period. The idea of heaven as the realm of God and its evil equivalent of hell was solidified because of Zoroastrianism. She'ol was a Netherworld that made sense in the context of other Near Eastern religions, including that of the conquering Babylonians, but with the Jews' knowledge of Persian dualism, She'ol no longer seemed logical.

The Jews of the Diaspora lived far from the land of Israel. As the years passed and their life in exile became more permanent, their religious ties to the land of Israel began to change, became more theoretical. The She'ol of the Bible was a very physical place, located under the Land of Israel itself. This is why it made much more sense for Diaspora Jews to think of life after death as a heaven or hell prospect, one that could take place anywhere, rather than as an underworld associated with a land they no longer lived in.

The concept of duality, and of a hell that is separate from the domain of God, solidified in Judaism during the Greek and Roman periods. Persian rule over the Jews ended when the Greeks conquered the Persians in the fourth century B.C.E. The Greeks in turn were conquered by the Romans, who took over the land of Israel in 40 B.C.E.

Much of the religious history of the Greek and Roman period comes down to us through the writings of the Jewish historian Josephus, who lived in the first century C.E.[5] In his writings, Josephus describes three main sects of Judaism, all of which developed during the Greek period, in the middle of the second century B.C.E.—the Pharisees, the Sadducees, and the Essenes.

The Pharisees and the Sadducees both came into existence precisely during the period of the Maccabean revolt against the Greeks that is memorialized by the Jewish holiday Chanukah. This timing is not a coincidence, as the Jews not only protested Greek political rule, they also had terrible trouble adapting to the presence of Greek ideas and cultural aspects. In fact, the knowledge of these untenable Greek ideas helped to solidify certain aspects of Jewish religion for each of the sects.

The Pharisees appear in the New Testament as well as in Josephus. Mark harshly criticizes the Pharisees for caring more about the letter of the law than about loving God, and for opposing Jesus (Mark 7.1). The term Pharisee is thought to come from the Hebrew word meaning "to separate," although it is not at all clear that this sect separated itself from the masses. In fact the Pharisees seemed to have embraced the masses, interpreting the law in such a way that allowed all groups of Jews to participate in ritual life.

According to Josephus, the Pharisees were interested in preserving ancient traditions and imparting them to all the Jews. Beyond this, they believed in the validity of the Oral Law, then already being composed in the rabbinic academies. The Oral Law was in its infancy during the Greek period but would later grow and become the Talmud of the Jews.

The Pharisees most fully embraced the ideas concerning death borrowed from Persian Zoroastrianism. They believed in an afterlife beyond this life, one filled with divine retribution—God would reward or punish people in the afterlife for their deeds in this life. The Pharisees also believed in angels and demons. Both angels and demons appear in the Hebrew Bible, but these sorts of beings had much greater importance in Zoroastrian beliefs.

The Sadducees were in direct opposition to the Pharisees. The Sadducees were aristocrats—the priestly class. The term Sadducee is thought to derive from the name Zaddok, who was the first High Priest of the Temple of Solomon. The Sadducees took no stock in the Oral Law. They did not believe in an afterlife at all, let alone one with divine retribution, claiming that God accounted for their actions in this life. They did not believe in angels or demons.

The Sadducees disappeared shortly after the Romans destroyed the Second Temple in 70 C.E. Because the priestly Sadducees considered themselves guardians of the Temple and its rites, their role in communal life ceased to exist without it.

The Pharisees, on the other hand, persisted after the destruction of 70 C.E. Pharisaic beliefs, including those concerning death and afterlife, evolved directly into the belief system of Rabbinic Judaism, which in turn led directly to that of modern Judaism.

The third sect described by Josephus was comprised of the Essenes, whose name means "purity" and who lived an almost monastic existence.[6] The Essenes believed that the Saduccaic priesthood was corrupt. They wanted to separate themselves from the priesthood as well as from the rest of the Jews. They considered themselves more holy than others. They referred to themselves as the "Sons of Light" and to members of other sects as the "Sons of Darkness," a duality very much in line with Zoroastrian beliefs. The Essenes shared the Pharisaic belief in an afterlife but did not survive much beyond the Roman destruction.

While all three of these sects were the result of the same period of religious and political ferment, only the ideas and beliefs of the Pharisees continued beyond antiquity. The Pharisees believed in an afterlife and associated ideas, and these ideas survived into later Judaism and Christianity as well.

The ideas of a heaven and a hell with divine retribution were highly appealing to Jews living in exile. Their Diaspora lives were fraught with difficulties, even persecutions; they could embrace the possibility of reward or even recompense in an afterlife.

The Metamorphosis of the Devil in Judeo-Christianity

The good/evil duality that came into Judaism with Persian Zoroastrianism paved the way for a devil, a being who personified evil, much the way God personified good. Before Zoroastrianism, there was no precedent for a devil in Near Eastern belief, only for underworld rulers.

On the other hand, Satan is a character in the Hebrew Bible. Satan, or more accurately, "the satan," is a member of God's heavenly court, one who acts as an adversary. The term "satan" is the Hebrew word for adversary and is used as such in several places in biblical narrative, often referring to an adversary in battle (see 1 Sam. 29.4).

The Bible puts Satan at the right hand of God in God's heavenly court, and treats him as a sort of angel—clearly as a member of God's entourage.

> Then he showed me . . . Satan standing at His [the Lord's] right hand . . . (Zech. 3.1)

> But God's anger was kindled . . . and the angel of the Lord took His stand in the way as His adversary [his satan] . . . (Num. 22.22)

The book of Job, written in the sixth century B.C.E. if not earlier, explores the adversarial role of Satan more fully than any other biblical source. In Job, Satan's relationship with God becomes clearer. The premise of Job is a test—can man keep his faith in God even in the face of terrible troubles? God gives Satan free rein to administer this test (Job 2.12), allowing him three opportunities to do whatever he wants to Job, short of killing him. Satan kills Job's family and makes Job very ill.

In response, Job curses the day he was born but never curses God, and stubbornly takes up a philosophical dialogue with three friends about his unwavering faith in God. In the end, God restores Job's good fortunes as a reward for his faith, in contrast to the lack of faith that his friends showed. The moral of the story is that nothing, not even Satan, can break man's faith in God.

In spite of the prefixed definite article that remains in front of his name, (the) Satan is present in this story as an actual, realized character, not just as an allegory for evil.

> Now there was a day when the sons of God came to present themselves before the Lord, and the Satan also came among them. The Lord said to the Satan, "Whence have you come?" The Satan answered the Lord, "From going to and fro on the earth, and from walking up and down it." And the Lord said to the Satan, "Have you considered my servant Job . . ." (Job 1.6–8)

Each time God talks to Satan he begins by asking him where he came from, and each time Satan replies that he has been wandering the earth. This gives us the idea that Satan lives with people when he is not doing God's bidding, which in turn leads to the later Judeo-Christian idea of Satan being able to tempt men to do evil.

These biblical references to Satan were interpreted in the light of the later dualist belief in good versus evil, and Satan neatly became the Judeo-Christian devil. In fact the term "devil" comes simply from the translation of "satan," adversary, into Greek as "diabolic." As the term evolved into English it was shortened to devil.

Beelzebub, another popular term for Satan, also comes from the Hebrew Bible. Beelzebub, or "ba'al zevuv," is Hebrew for Lord of the Flies, a derogatory name for the god of the Philistines, enemy of the Israelites. Another derogatory version of this name was Beelzebul, lord of garbage. As the belief in the devil became standard, these insulting names for a god of Israel's enemies were viewed as logical appellations for the opponent of God himself. The identification of Beelzebub with the devil was made as early as the first century C.E. as Matthew makes reference to "Beelzebul, the prince of demons" (Matt. 12.24).

The term Lucifer, a Latin term that comes from a translation of a Hebrew phrase, is another common term for the devil. Lucifer, which means "bearer of light," originated in a passage of Isaiah that was taken out of context.

> How you have fallen from Heaven, O Day Star, Son of Dawn. How you are cut down to the ground, you who laid the nations low. You said in your heart, I will ascend to heaven, above the stars of God, I will set my throne on

> high, I will sit on the mount of assembly in the far north. I will ascend above the heights of the clouds, I will make myself like the Most High. But you are brought down to She'ol, to the depths of the pit. (Isa. 14.12–15)

This passage is a taunt directed at the king of Babylon. Isaiah was written during the last years of the kingdom of Judah. In the sentences that precede this quote, Isaiah prophesied that even though Babylon will undoubtedly conquer Judah, the Babylonians themselves will eventually be overthrown, and at that point Judah will be able to taunt the king of Babylon (Isa. 14.3–4).

In this passage the taunted king of Babylon is referred to in his own language—that of royalty and divinity. This is why he is called "day star, son of dawn," as well as "you who laid the nations low." The phrase "day star," was translated into Latin as Lucifer (bearer of light). The passage begins by recounting the greatness of the Day Star, or Lucifer, and ends by saying that Lucifer will end up in She'ol—hell. This is the origin of the belief that the devil is not just an angel but a fallen angel, a belief that Christianity made popular.

During the Greek and Roman periods, the physical characteristics of the devil were borrowed from classical sources, most notably from mythological images. The god Pan was part goat, and the devil's cloven hooves and horns come from images of Pan as well as from more general images of Dionysiac satyrs.

Even though hell and the devil were created through a conflation of Hebrew, Persian, and classical traditions, Jewish practices relating to death did not change very much in these early years. Jews in Judea (as Israel was then called) still buried their dead in acrosolia, which were still used for entire family groups. The family tombs of the Israelites persisted.

But as Diaspora life became the norm for the Jews, and as belief in an afterlife that was not physically located became part of Jewish ideology, a related belief, one that had received little attention in the biblical world, suddenly took center stage. This was the belief in bodily resurrection.

6

Resurrection and Lack of Death in the Bible

As foreign as it might sound to modern ears, the idea of the dead coming to life again has very firm roots in Judaism. Resurrection has always been a Jewish belief, and Orthodox Jews today still recite a daily prayer, "Blessed be God, who resurrects the dead."

Like most aspects of funerary beliefs and practices, the belief in resurrection can be traced from the Bible and archaeology of the biblical period, through the Rabbinic period, and into modern times. Like the evolution of the biblical Netherworld into a much more abstract afterlife, resurrection changed in reaction to the changing situation of the Jews as they moved from the Land of Israel to Diaspora communities.

Resurrection evolved from being a nebulous and tangential belief in the biblical world to a very concrete and central belief in the world of early Judaism. In fact the belief in bodily resurrection was so central to Judaism by the later Middle Ages that any expression of doubts regarding it was actually considered heretical.

Resurrection in the Hebrew Bible

The Israelites regularly opened the tombs of their fathers and regularly handled and rearranged the desiccated bones of family members. Did they actually believe that these fleshless bones would turn into living, breathing people again? The answer is no. The Israelites did not believe in resurrection the way the later rabbis thought they did.

While there are several stories in the Hebrew Bible involving resurrection, the most interesting discussion of the topic is within the context of a prophecy, not a narrative text. The prophecy is in the book of Ezekiel. God told Ezekiel that a day will come when sinews and flesh will grow onto the bones of all the generations of dead Israelites, and they will live again.

> He said to me, "O, mortal, can these bones live again?"
>
> I replied, "O Lord God, only You know."
>
> And He said to me, "Prophesy over these bones and say to them: O dry bones, hear the word of the Lord! Thus said the Lord God to these bones: I will cause breath to enter you and you shall live again. I will lay sinews upon you, and cover you with flesh, and form skin over you, and I will put breath into you, and you shall live again. And you shall know that I am the Lord."
>
> So I prophesied as I was commanded, and as I prophe-

> sied, there was a noise, and behold, a rattling, and the bones came together, bone to its bone. And as I looked, there were sinews on them, and flesh had come upon them, and skin had covered them, but there was no breath in them.
>
> Then he said to me, "Prophesy to the breath, prophesy, son of man, and say to the breath, Thus says the Lord God: Come from the four winds, O breath, and breathe upon these slain, that they may live."
>
> So I prophesied as he commanded me, and the breath came into them, and they lived, and stood upon their feet, an exceedingly great host. Then he said to me, Son of Man, these bones are the whole House of Israel. (Ezek. 37.3–11)

This passage protests almost too much. The Israelites knew what bones looked like and knew how the process of decay worked. Ezekiel actually reverses the processes of decay from the bones outward, as if explaining to people who were already aware of the physical truths of death that this was not just a vague vision but a specific one. You do not think that God can do this, he seems to be saying. Well, this is exactly how God will put the bones back together.

The prophetic context of the description also implies that the Israelites did not think resurrection was an immediate possibility. In spite of the specific nature of this description, the dry bones vision is clearly an event for some other time and place.

Ezekiel also clearly intends this vision of resurrection to apply to all the dead of Israel together. This is not a vision that gives immediate comfort to the individual or even to the individual family. It does not imply that one's own death, or that of a specific family member, can be reversed. It is much more theoretical and long term than that.

The other references to resurrection in the Hebrew Bible also demonstrate that resurrection was not an important part of the Israelite belief system. Even what seems to be a clear example is not really clear at all. Here is a story from the life of the prophet Elisha.

> When Elisha came into the house, he saw the child lying dead on his bed. So he went in and shut the door upon the two of them, and prayed to the Lord. Then he went up and lay upon the child, putting his mouth upon his mouth, his eyes upon his eyes and his hands upon his hands, and as he stretched himself upon him, the flesh of the child became warm. Then he got up again and walked once to and fro in the house and went up and stretched himself upon him; the child sneezed seven times and the child opened his eyes. (2 Kings 4.32–35)

This narrative describes a prophet bringing a child back to life. The fact that Elisha is a prophet stands out right away. Circumstances must be right for someone to be resurrected. In this case the child's mother knew Elisha, and he had promised to help her. In other words, Elisha was not about to revive every dead person he encountered.

A modern reading of this passage can easily reconfigure it into one of resuscitation, not revivification. Elisha was called immediately after the child collapsed—as if it were an emergency and the child could only be "brought back to life" if action were taken right away. It seems that the child merely stopped breathing and that Elisha performed mouth-to-mouth resuscitation on him.

In short, this story is about the revival of someone who was close to death but who had not died, not about the revival of a person dead for a long time. Although the story was marketed as one of resurrection, even the Israelites must have understood the differences.

Besides resuscitating this child, Elisha performs one more resurrection, this one after he himself is dead.

> So Elisha died and they buried him. Now bands of Moabites used to invade the land in the spring of the year. And as a man was being buried, lo, a marauding band was seen and the man was cast into the grave of Elisha; and as soon as the man touched the bones of Elisha, he revived and stood on his feet. (2 Kings 13.20–21)

When a body is thrown into the grave of Elisha and touches Elisha's bones, the body comes alive again. This reference is unambiguous, but it is told with no realistic details, making it very unlike the other references to resurrection. We do not know how long this body has been dead, nor do we know the circumstances of death. Because of the lack of details, the reader is supposed to believe the story without asking questions.

This leap of faith makes the story stand out as folklore, especially when compared to Elisha's more realistic resurrection/resuscitation of the child. A likely scenario is that since Elisha had once brought a child back to life, he acquired the reputation of having the power of resurrection, and the later story was made up from whole cloth.

Besides the biblical stories, which cast Israelite belief in resurrection in a doubtful light at best, the archaeological evidence from Israelite tombs confirms that the Israelites did not believe in resurrection as a realistic possibility. The Israelites regularly put capping stones over their tombs. This sealed the tombs, preventing anything from entering or exiting. Sealing tombs was necessary for several reasons. It served as a (slight) deterrent against tomb robbers and also contained the odor of decomposition. Tombs were reopened only when family members needed to deposit an additional body inside, and their capping stones were afterward replaced.

Not only is there physical evidence for capping stones, there is textual references to them as well, from both the Hebrew Bible and the New Testament.

> But at the time of the going down of the sun, Joshua commanded, and they took them down from the trees, and threw them into the cave where they had hidden themselves, and they set great stones against the mouth of the cave, which remain to this very day. (Josh. 11.27)

If resurrection were an actual possibility, the Israelites would not seal off their tombs, as the capping stones make it impossible for a body to leave the tomb after resurrection. Had the Israelites believed that those bodies were going anywhere, they would have made provisions for them to do so. They believed in the need of the dead to eat, so they left food offerings.

Had they believed in the need of the dead to leave the tomb once revived, they would have left an opening in the tomb.

The fact that they left no such openings, combined with the textual doubt discussed above, leads to the inevitable conclusion that the Israelites did not truly believe in resurrection, certainly not as a real possibility for the immediate future, though they may have already spoken of it in prayers.

Resurrection in the New Testament

The New Testament, the Bible of a religion that itself is predicated on the resurrection of Jesus, contains stories of resurrection of a very different sort than those in the Hebrew Bible. Both the two New Testament resurrection stories are about resurrections of someone dead for a long time and therefore attest to a clearer power of resurrection. Here is the resurrection of Lazarus:

> Then Jesus . . . came to the tomb; it was a cave and a stone lay upon it. Jesus said "Take away the stone." Martha, the sister of the dead man, said to him, "Lord, by this time there will be an odor, for he has been dead four days." . . . So they took away the stone. And Jesus lifted up his eyes and said, "Father I thank thee that thou hast heard me. . . ." When he had said this, he cried with a loud voice, "Lazarus, come out." The dead man came out, his hands and feet bound with bandages, and his face wrapped with a cloth. Jesus said to them, "Unbind him, and let him go." (John 11.38–44)

The story emphasizes the fact that Lazarus has been dead a while. Not only has his tomb already been sealed with a capping stone, but his sister, doubting Jesus' power, specifically points out that decomposition will already have begun—"there will be an odor, for he has been dead four days." Nonetheless Jesus brings him back to life, proving that this is a real resurrection, not like those of the Hebrew Bible.

Jesus' own resurrection is similar. According to the various versions (Matt. 28, Mark 18, Luke 14, John 20), Joseph of Arimathea takes Jesus' body and places it in a rock-hewn tomb, which he caps with a stone. When visitors bring spices to the tomb several days after his burial, they find the tomb open and his body gone. Later they encounter Jesus himself, alive again.

As in the case of Lazarus (and in spite of the differences in details) there is no question that time has elapsed between death and resurrection. Jesus "escapes" from a closed tomb and does so three full days after his death, making it clear that this is a miraculous resurrection, not like the more "natural" one performed by Elisha in the Hebrew Bible.

The Gospels of Matthew and John both end with Jesus still resurrected—they do not specifically state where he went afterward, why he is no longer in the world now, or why he (therefore) must come again. Mark and Luke, on the other hand, state that after he spoke to the people, Jesus "was taken up to heaven, and sat at the right hand of God" (Mark 16.19; Luke 24.51). The language of this phrase, "taken up to heaven," is reminiscent of the Old Testament disappearance of Elijah.

Thus while the Israelites did not believe in physical resurrection per se (though they retained it as a divine possibility), the early Christians made actual resurrections an integral part of their religion.

Lack of Death in the Hebrew Bible

A concept related to resurrection is lack of death. There are two instances in the Hebrew Bible when a person simply does not die; instead he joins God while still alive.

The first instance of lack of death is from the book of Genesis. According to the traditional Jewish interpretation of the biblical text, Enoch, a man mentioned in a few sentences in Genesis, never died. The tradition of Enoch's nondeath comes from the following verses:

> When Enoch had lived 65 years, he begot Methuselah. After the birth of Methuselah, Enoch walked with God 300 years; and he begot sons and daughters. All the days of Enoch came to 365 years. Enoch walked with God; then he was no more, for God took him (Gen. 5.21–24)

The phrase "then he was no more" is what makes Enoch's death into a nondeath. The Hebrew "einenu" is not used elsewhere in the Hebrew Bible concerning death, and therefore the rabbis of the Talmud, who held the view that every word in the Hebrew Bible was inspired by God, took this unique expression to mean that Enoch did not die but rather entered the realm of God without dying.

The argument hinges on the repeated use of the phrase "walked with God." Why would the Bible use the very same phrase when Enoch was clearly still alive, then use it again just before God takes him? The answer, according to the rabbis, is that he did not die.

Another interpretation, however, is that both "walked with God" and "he was no more" are stray phrases, devoid of great meaning. The second "walked with God" could merely refer to the last bit of time that Enoch was alive, and the phrase "he was no more" could simply be an unusual way of saying that he died. Therefore Enoch is not a clear-cut case of lack of death.

The more famous case of biblical lack of death concerns the prophet Elijah, who ascends to heaven in a fiery chariot, right in front of an eyewitness. This miraculous disappearance from the world is still memorialized in the Jewish holiday Passover, when a cup of wine is left out for Elijah, who is vaguely thought to be "out there" (since he is not dead) and therefore should be able to make stops in the homes of living people.

The story takes up most of Chapter 2 of 2 Kings. In this chapter, Elijah the prophet and his protégé Elisha walk together from town to town. During this walk both men seem to be aware that God will imminently "take Elijah up to heaven in a whirlwind" (2 Kings 2.1). Elijah asks Elisha not to continue on with him, but Elisha insists on continuing. Furthermore the people they meet in each town remind Elisha that God is about to take Elijah away.

When the two men reach the Jordan River, Elijah magically parts the water so they can cross. He then asks Elisha what he can do for him "before I am taken from you" (v. 9). Elisha says that he would like to inherit "a double share of [your] spirit" (v. 10). Elijah replies that if Elisha sees him being taken, it will mean that he will get his wish.

> As they kept on walking and talking, a fiery chariot with fiery horses suddenly appeared and separated one from the other, and Elijah went up to heaven in a whirlwind. Elisha saw it and he cried out, "Oh father, father! Israel's chariots and horsemen!" When he could no longer see him, he grasped his garments, and rent them in two. (2 Kings 2.1, 11–12)

The narrative continues after the remarkable departure of Elijah. Elisha retraces their steps and then parts the Jordan River just as Elijah had done earlier, a sign that Elisha had in fact received the double share of Elijah's spirit.

Elisha's tearing of clothes is one of the signs of mourning used in the Bible from the time of Jacob's mourning for Joseph. This does not mean that Elijah died, only that Elisha acknowledges that he is permanently gone, and that he is with God, two circumstances that are common to death as well as to this disappearance. Because the event is unique and therefore suggests no set rituals to go along with it, Elisha engages in death rituals as the closest known behavior.

One thing to point out about this narrative is that both men knew in advance that Elijah would be taken by God in this unusual manner. It is completely unclear what is meant by the phrase "in a whirlwind," though images of a twister tornado and Dorothy's trip to Oz permeate the modern reading of the phrase.

Another interesting piece of this narrative is what Elisha

calls out when Elijah goes up in the whirlwind. "My father" could either refer to Elijah his mentor or to God himself, but the puzzling phrase is "Israel's chariots and horsemen." It seems that Elisha sees Israel's chariots and horsemen in the whirlwind. (This is somewhat reminiscent of a later passage in the Bible, when Ezekiel sees a divine chariot.) Elisha's vision, it should be remembered, did not have to do with death but with nondeath.

The messianic view of resurrection confuses the issue yet again. When the Judahites were first conquered by the Babylonians and exiled to Babylon, they fervently hoped and believed that it was a temporary situation. They believed that God would imminently restore them to Jerusalem, and that they would have a king again very soon.

A tradition regarding kings in ancient Israel, as well as in most other parts of the ancient world, was that new kings would be anointed with oil as a symbol of taking on kingship. An alternate Hebrew term for king was "anointed one," in Hebrew, "Messiah."[1] The idea of the Messiah coming was a realistic one in those early days of exile.

By the Rabbinic period it was clear that the Judahite kingdom would not be restored—there would be no Messiah in the immediate future. The concept of the Messiah evolved from the realm of immediate possibility into an end-of-days eschatology. Eventually the Messiah will come, and the world as we know it will end, and at that point the predictions of Ezekiel will be fulfilled. Among other things that will happen at the time of the Messiah, the dead will be revived.

This messianic philosophy is part of both Judaism and

Christianity.[2] And the following questions apply to the messianic raising of the dead in both religions: Once the dead are revived, what happens afterward? Do people no longer die—do they no longer experience an afterlife in the realm of God? Or do people continue to die, and those who have been resurrected later die a second time?

During the Middle Ages this question was impossible to answer, as Judaism had completely conflated the tenet of afterlife with that of resurrection. The rabbinic interpretation of a very late biblical text was partly responsible for this conflation. The Book of Daniel, codified as part of the Hebrew Bible though it was written in the second century B.C.E., during the Hellenistic period, contains the following sentence:

> And many of those who sleep in the dust of the earth shall awake, some to everlasting life, and some to shame and everlasting contempt. (Dan. 12.2)

According to this passage, many, but not necessarily all, of the dead will be resurrected. Presumably those who are not resurrected will continue in an afterlife, while those who are resurrected will not die again but in fact will be immortal. Rabbinic reliance on this passage confused the two issues irreparably.

When the twelfth-century exegete Maimonides tried to unravel resurrection from afterlife, he was posthumously excommunicated by the Jewish community for his heretical beliefs. Maimonides himself believed that there would be a second death after resurrection and also dared to doubt the actuality of bodily resurrection.

Clearly, by the beginning of the Rabbinic period, Judaism had fully endorsed the tenet of resurrection, even though a close reading of the biblical texts makes it clear that the Israelites themselves had not believed in it.

The Jews of the later periods were looking toward the Messiah, and toward resurrection in the time of the Messiah, as a way of getting past the persecutions they faced in their everyday lives on earth. Belief in ultimate resurrection, as well as in heavenly afterlife, gave them something to look forward to. This is why they held up resurrection as an integral tenet of Judaism. Resurrection became a central part of their religious agenda, and they read the Bible with this agenda in mind.

7

Death in Rabbinic Judaism

Once the world had settled into the late classical and early Christian periods, how did Jewish death look? How did the Jews resolve their newer beliefs and newest political and religious conflicts into the ancient funerary rites they still practiced? Did they abandon some death or burial practices, or did they add new ones to reflect their new beliefs about afterlife?

The answers to these questions can be found in the Talmud. The term Talmud comes from the Aramaic and Hebrew root lamad, meaning to study or learn. The Talmud is the result of generations of argument and explanation in the rabbinic academies in Palestine and Babylon. It was composed between the first century B.C.E. and the fifth century C.E., spanning the Roman and early Christian periods of rule in Palestine and the Parthian and Sassanian periods in Babylon.

For modern Orthodox and Conservative Jews today, the

Talmud is still the law. Modern rabbis extrapolate upon Talmudic laws when necessary but never abandon them—for instance, observant Jews do not use electricity on the Sabbath because Rabbinic period laws stated that fire should not be used or moved on the Sabbath.

It is commonly believed that rabbinic laws derive from biblical laws, but this is not entirely accurate. A more realistic view is that the laws of the Talmud are reflections of the living customs of the Jewish communities of the Talmudic period.

While the Bible is certainly the basis for the laws of the Talmud, Talmudic laws are only dimly related to biblical ones. Most passages of the Mishnah, the earliest part of the Talmud, begin by simply stating a law, then give examples of how that law is applied to daily life. In most cases the Bible is not mentioned at all. When the rabbis of the latter part of the Talmud elaborated on such laws, they looked to the Bible to find a text that would support the laws and customs; but these texts served as justifications, not explanations.

How can this be? How can the main legal treatise of Judaism have so few direct references to the laws of the Pentateuch—the first five books of the Bible?

There is a gap in Jewish textual material between the Bible and the Talmud. The gap extends for two hundred to three hundred years.[1] During this time, laws evolved to meet the needs of the various Diaspora communities in all their countries and situations. Through information gathered from the writings of Josephus and the New Testament, we have already seen how beliefs concerning death and afterlife evolved during these years, and the ways that these beliefs solidified in the following centuries.

By the time the gap in Jewish textual evidence ends and the Talmud begins, something extraordinary has happened, concerning not only death beliefs but the religion as a whole: the ancient religion of the Israelites has changed almost beyond recognition. These "people from Judah" (Jews), as they were referred to in Babylon, were no longer attached to their land, but their religion still reflected its ancient origins, even as it was grounded in the present situation.

This is why the death customs of the Talmudic period look so different from those of the biblical period. Not only were the concepts of the afterlife and resurrection fully developed by the time the textual gap ends, folk customs and superstitions concerning death and afterlife had developed in the interim as well.

Death, Burial, and Afterlife in the Talmud

While the Talmud may mention a particular custom or belief as if it were universally accepted, some customs and beliefs may actually have been only regional phenomena. These regional customs became universally accepted later, and then only due to Talmudic mentions themselves.

The rabbis of the Talmud knew about the mourning rituals of their own communities. These rituals had developed over generations, borrowing traditions from local populations and adding them into their own ancient ones. When the rabbis of the Talmudic period read the Bible, their holy text, they already had these community rituals in mind. This is why they emphasized only those biblical death customs that their communities were already practicing.

The following is a list of biblical references to mourning practices, all of which are also discussed in the Talmud: tearing clothes, wearing sackcloth or mourning robes, wearing garments of widowhood, removing embroidered garments, putting dust on the head, fasting, beating the breast, wailing, covering the hair, not cutting the hair or shaving, cutting, gashing, making incisions on the hands or elsewhere, tattooing, covering the upper lip, not eating meat, not drinking wine, not dancing, not playing instrumental music, not exchanging gifts, reciting lamentations.

Some of these mourning rituals receive only brief mentions in the Bible. An example is the cutting of the hands, known only from negative commandments—"You shall not make any cuttings in your flesh on account of the dead or tattoo any marks upon you" (Lev. 19.28).

Others are mentioned repeatedly in the Bible, such as the tearing of clothes. The earliest such mention is a Joseph story that is not about a real death at all, as Jacob only believes Joseph is dead when he is not. Although the tradition originated with mourning a man who was not yet dead, tearing clothes as a sign of mourning came down into rabbinic tradition—and from there into modern Jewish custom—as an extremely important mourning rite.

In spite of the fact that so many different ways of expressing grief are mentioned in the Bible—there are more than twenty on the list above—the Talmudic rabbis had preconceived ideas of what mourning rituals were important and appropriate.

Talmudic Laws and Practices Concerning Death

One of the most unusual facets of Talmudic death practices is that death is almost never mentioned directly in any of the prayers sanctioned for mourning and burial.

The main prayer said by mourners is the "Mourners' Kaddish." Kaddish means sanctification, and this prayer is one that praises God. Its text is as follows:

> May God's great name be magnified and sanctified. In this world, which He has created in accordance with His will, may he establish His kingdom during your lifetime, and during the life of all the house of Israel, speedily. And let us say, Amen.
>
> Let His great name be blessed forever and to all eternity.
>
> Blessed, praised, glorified, exalted, extolled, honored, magnified, and lauded, by the name of the Holy One, blessed be He.
>
> He is greater than all blessings, hymns, praises, and consolations which can be uttered in this world.
>
> May abundant peace from heaven descend upon us and may life be renewed for us and for all Israel.
>
> He who makes peace in the heavens, may He make peace for us and for all Israel.

This Mourners' Kaddish is recited by Jewish mourners several times a day, from the day of the death until a year following the death.[2] But the only near-mention it makes of mourning is its declaration that God is greater than consolation, a rather oblique consolation for the mourner.

This is because the Kaddish is not meant to comfort the mourner at all. Instead Kaddish is supposed to remind the mourner that God knows what He is doing—in his grief, a mourner might not be able to comprehend why his loved one has died, but in spite of this he should still remember that this death is a part of God's mysterious plan, which humans cannot understand. All we can do is praise God and accept His judgment.

The only time anything directly relating to death is added to this Kaddish is at the gravesite itself. There one recites the "Burial Kaddish," which has several extra lines including,

> May His great name be magnified and sanctified, in the world which He will renew, reviving the dead and raising them to life eternal.

Death is mentioned at the time of burial, but only then. But even this Burial Kaddish does not emphasize the loss, the actual death, but the fact that God will revive all the dead. In the Talmudic world, the deeply held, barely biblical belief in resurrection superceded the need to comfort the individual mourner.

Although death plays such a minor part in the verbal part of mourning, elaborate customs developed in the Talmudic period concerning both death and dying. These customs make clear that Talmudic period Jews considered a dying man to be in close proximity to God already.

According to the Talmud, one is allowed to violate the sabbath in order to make a dying man more comfortable. The implications of this ruling are profound, as one is allowed to break the Sabbath only to do God's work, for instance to save a life. This ruling, that the Sabbath could be broken to help a dying man, means that people considered dying a holy act, or at the very least an act that brought the dying individual closer to God.

If the dying man was considered to be close to God, he needed to be treated differently from an ordinary man. This is why the rabbis of the Talmud considered it a positive commandment (mitzvah) to be present at the moment of death.

When a man lay on his deathbed, his relatives would place a candle near him to symbolize the flickering of his soul. They would encourage him to confess his sins so that he could receive a portion in the next world. This is akin to modern Christian death practices, where a person can still save his soul by repenting on his deathbed.

Several specific requirements had to be met before death was determined in the Rabbinic period. Death was confirmed when breathing, pulse, heartbeat, and corneal reflex all ceased. These functions were checked and double checked—a feather was placed on the lips, and the body was not touched for eight minutes. The feather was watched intently during the eight minutes, and if there was no breath to move it, death was then established.

The fact that not just one but several bodily functions had to stop before death was confirmed attests to a strong fear of false death within the Talmudic communities. In fact the grave itself was watched for a full three days after burial in case of pseudo-death.[3] This fear of being buried while still alive was one of the reasons why a corpse was never allowed to be alone, in case the person "woke up." Other reasons for the constant presence of a guard from the moment of death until the funeral were to honor the dead and to protect the corpse from harm (either malicious or from animals).

As soon as death was established, someone closed the eyes and mouth of the corpse and extended its arms and hands. The point of this was to allow the body the respect it deserved. The body was then placed on the floor and covered by a sheet. It was always placed with its feet facing the door, reflecting a superstition that impurities could exit from the feet. The guards would place a candle near the head and keep the candle burning from the time of death until the funeral.

Talmudic legend emphasizes that death was sanctioned by God at the creation of the world. This emphasis on the inevitability of death in part compensates for the lack of consolation language in mourning prayers.

According to one legend, every human knows all the wisdom and knowledge in the world when he is in the womb, but immediately before birth the Angel of Death touches him in the middle of his upper lip (leaving the slight cleft as a scar), and at that moment he forgets everything and must start from scratch.[4] Another legend says that the Angel of Death was present on the day of Creation. A third, unrelated Talmudic saying concerning both birth and death is as follows: Man is born with his fists tightly clenched, saying, "The whole world is mine," but he dies with his hands open, saying, "I have inherited (taken) nothing from the world."

All three of these passages turn death into something natural within the Talmudic mind-set—since the Angel of Death is present at both the beginning of the world and at the beginnings of individual lives, he is expected to return at the end of life (and at the end of the world) as well.

Another selection from the Talmud describes how the Angel of Death operates. A person sees the Angel of Death whose eyes are of coal and who carries a sword. When the person opens his mouth to shriek in fear, the Angel of Death drops some gall (bile) into his mouth. According to this story, the gall not only causes death, it also explains why a decaying corpse has an odor.

The Talmud also states that at the moment of death a righteous man can see the Divine Presence, that is, God. And the tractate Yoma (from the Talmud) says that the soul leaves the body with a cry that reverberates around the world.

The Talmud differentiates between types of death. Righteous men die with the "kiss of death"—a gentle, easy death in their sleep. The Talmud also considers death on the Sabbath a good sort of death. This is contrasted with the worst types of death, including deaths from asthma and croup. Oddly, deaths from diseases of the bowels, which entailed much suffering, were considered good.

Funeral and Burial in the Talmud

By the late Rabbinic period, people would pour out all the drawn water in the vicinity of the house of the death. A traditional explanation for this folk custom is that pouring water was a way of announcing the death without verbally declaring bad news.

While nonverbal announcement is clearly in the realm of superstition, rabbinic literature offers a prooftext for this. (A prooftext is a text taken from the Bible to prove a point.) In the Bible, Moses' sister Miriam died while the Israelites were wandering in the Sinai desert. Following her death, there was no water. Perhaps the tradition of pouring out water as a way of announcing death was originally a way of implying that the deceased was an important person in the community, as important as Miriam.

Preparations for burial began soon after death. The body needed to be ritually purified before burial, based on two separate and unrelated biblical verses.

> I will sprinkle clean water upon you and you shall be clean from all your uncleannesses . . . (Ezek. 36.25)

> As he came from his mother's womb, so he shall go again, naked as he came, and shall take nothing for his toil which he may carry away in his hand. (Eccles. 5.15)

Although the first verse does not refer specifically to washing the dead, and the second verse does not refer to washing, the two were conflated in the Talmud as prooftexts to account for the traditional cleansing of the corpse.

This is a typical Talmudic use of prooftexts. In spite of the fact that the biblical text never mentions that people washed corpses before burying them, and in spite of the fact that there is no evidence that any such custom was part of Israelite custom, the rabbis found justification for washing—one of their own established folk customs—in their holy Bible.

A quorum of men (or women, depending on the sex of the deceased), called a Hevra Kaddisha, was responsible for preparing the body. These groups still exist in almost all Jewish communities today. The term is generally translated as "burial society," although a more accurate translation would be "group involved in holy work." These people would place the corpse on a board, feet still facing the door. They would then clean the body with lukewarm water while reciting biblical verses such as Ezekiel 36.25 (above).

After they cleaned the body with water, they would rub the head and front part of the body with a beaten egg. The egg, because of its shape, was the traditional symbol of the perpetuity of life (which is why it appears in the springtime holidays of both Passover and Easter). Next the burial workers would pour nine measures (4.5 gallons) of water over the body while holding it in an upright position. They then dried it and dressed it in shrouds.

The process was more elaborate for a great rabbi. In some communities the body of such a rabbi was even dipped in the waters of the ritual bathhouse.

After they finished the cleaning, the participants would wash their hands with salted water as a step toward purifying themselves from contact with the dead body.

In Rabbinic Jewish tradition, burial had to take place within a day after the death. This was at least partly a response to the warm climate of the Middle East, where decomposition would occur soon after death.

The simplicity of Jewish coffins dates to the early-second-century sage Rabbi Gamliel, who saw them as more respectful to the dead than ostentatious ones, and also saw them as a way of differentiating Jewish burials from Christian ones.[5] Another Talmudic sage called Levi added a second reason to use plain wood coffins. The Talmud (not the Bible) says that after committing their sin, Adam and Eve tried to hide from God in the trees of the Garden of Eden. Therefore coffins for man's ultimate death should be of wood from trees. This, while several steps removed from any actual biblical story, is another example of the Talmud using the Bible as justification for a custom already in practice.

While the burial always remained simple, the ancient practice of putting grave goods into the grave or coffin persisted into the Talmudic period. In the Talmudic period this had become more ritualized than in the biblical period—specific items were left with specific individuals. For instance, a pen and some ink were placed near a bridegroom, and a key and a book of accounts were placed near a childless man. The latter tradition may reflect the tasks usually done by survivors of the deceased—if there were no sons to take care of his accounts and affairs after his death, he had to keep these items himself.

Food offerings as well as offerings of personal effects are attested in Jewish burials during the time of the Mishnah, the first part of the Talmud. This custom, so long-lived that it preceded the Israelites, took a long time to disappear.

According to the Talmud, it is a positive commandment to accompany a funeral procession. Therefore, in many towns in Talmudic times, the entire Jewish community would participate in the funeral.

Besides the procession, Jewish funerals in the Talmudic period continued several other ancient traditions, some of which are known specifically from the biblical world. The most striking of these is the use of professional mourners. These paid professionals were always women. They would accompany the procession to the burial site and would lead the public grieving with rhythmic hand-clapping, responsive dirges, and lamentations recited in unison.

Pallbearers would carry the coffin on their shoulders during the procession. The pallbearers were members of the Hevra Kaddisha. As they carried the coffin, they would recite prayers in praise of God, such as, "The Rock, His work is perfect, for all His ways are judgment." This, like the Mourners' Kaddish, was a way of reconciling one's grief to the religion—though you have experienced a loss, God knows better and has His reasons for causing this death.

The walk to the grave was interrupted with several stops, either five or seven, depending on regional variants of the tradition. At each stop the mourners would recite Psalm 91—another prayer in praise of God that also does not specifically refer to death. Psalm 23, which only briefly mentions the "valley of the shadow of death," is another option for funeral recitation.

Finally the mourners would recite the Burial Kaddish, with its mention of the ultimate resurrection of the dead. Then the mourners themselves would fill the grave with earth, completing the burial.

Mourning in the Talmud

The Rabbis of the Talmud decided that there were seven relationships that deserved official mourning. They loosely based this decision, as they did others, on various biblical passages.

One should mourn for the following seven relationships: one's mother, father, sister, brother, son, daughter, and spouse. But there are exceptions to this rule. Teachers and scholars may be mourned according to the same rules as close kin. In fact the Mourners' Kaddish originated as a prayer that one said after the conclusion of a study session led by a renowned scholar. From there it evolved into a prayer said at the death of such a scholar, and eventually became a required prayer for anyone mourning any death.

In the Bible there are instances of many different lengths of time for mourning. Joseph mourned his father Jacob for seven days after transporting him to Canaan but before burying him (Gen. 50.10). The people of Israel mourned Aaron for thirty days (Num. 20.29) and Moses for thirty days (Deut. 34.8). Daniel mourned an unspecified person for three weeks (Dan.

10.2). And Deuteronomy 21.13 mentions a captured gentile woman who mourns her parents for a month.

The rabbis of the Talmud brought these references into their discussions of mourning as prooftexts, but the length of mourning was well established from the beginning of the Talmudic period, if not earlier. Within Rabbinic Judaism there are four stages of mourning, each less intense than the previous.

The first stage, called Aninut (meaning "mourning"), is the period between the death itself and the burial. This is the most intense stage, where the mourner is responsible only for negative commandments ("Thou shalt not"), not positive ones such as the putting on of phylacteries. This is because the mourner is so distraught over the death at this stage that he cannot do anything else. Practically, it allows time to prepare for the burial.

The second stage of mourning is called Shiva, from the Hebrew word for seven. Shiva lasts seven days from the time of burial. There are several justifications given in the Talmud for the seven-day period—one is that God waited seven days after Methuselah died before making the Flood.

During Shiva the mourners are supposed to gather in the house of the deceased, sit on overturned couches and beds as a sign of distress, tear their garments, and recite a prayer similar to the Mourners' Kaddish, which praises God as the true judge (or as the judge of truth, depending on how the phrase is translated). During this period the mourners are not supposed to leave the house, engage in manual labor, engage in business, bathe, cut their hair, engage in sexual relations, wear leather, wash their clothes, greet people, prepare food, or study Torah, except for sorrowful portions such as the book of Job, Lamentations, or Jeremiah. The first three of these seven days were considered the most intense.

During both Aninut and Shiva the mourner does not eat meat, indulge by overeating, or drink wine, except on the Sabbath. Forgoing luxuries such as meat and wine was a sign of respect for the dead—one is too distraught to engage in such pleasures.

The next stage is called Sheloshim, from the Hebrew word for thirty. Sheloshim is a thirty-day period after the death and including the seven days of Shiva in which the mourner may not cut his hair, wear ironed clothes, marry or attend weddings, go to places of entertainment, or take business trips. In a few places these restrictions applied to the entire first year after the death. Both Shiva and Sheloshim could be annulled if they were interrupted by a holiday.

Talmudic mourning becomes less intense after Sheloshim, based on a single, somewhat misinterpreted and abbreviated biblical prooftext. Jeremiah 22.10 states,

> Weep not for him who is dead, nor bemoan him.

Within folk tradition this was interpreted as meaning that too much weeping might bring on another death. In fact the full verse in Jeremiah reads,

> Weep not for him who is dead, nor bemoan him, but weep bitterly for him who goes away, for he shall return no more to see his native land.

This is a direct reference to the Babylonian Exile of 586 B.C.E., an event that Jeremiah witnessed firsthand. For Jeremiah, being taken away to Babylon was a fate worse than death (Jeremiah himself escaped the Babylonians and fled to Egypt where he lived out his life), but the rabbis took this verse out of its context and used it as a justification for the already extant custom of decreasing degrees of mourning.

The Burial and Mourning of Children in the Talmud

Death practices in the ancient world differed according to status—high-status individuals might receive more elaborate burial treatments than low-status ones. Differing burial treatments based on status explains the "missing" burials of the biblical period—some burials were so simple that they are not visible in the archaeological record.

The rabbis of the Talmud made similar differentiations based on status, differentiations that are visible in the burial and mourning practices of nonadults. Although they would not have classed these differences as status-based, that is exactly what they are—children had a different role in Jewish society than adults, a very minimal role, and their burial and mourning treatment reflected this minimal role exactly.

Children were mourned with only a fraction of the ceremonies that were accorded to adults. This reflects the realities of a high infant mortality rate and Talmudic society's strategy for dealing with it. Rather than dwelling on the sadness of such a death, these deaths were given less attention than those of adults, most likely because infant death was so common that dwelling on such deaths would paralyze families. Spending less time grieving, and abbreviating the funeral ceremonies, forced parents and other family members to "get on with things" and return to regular life after such an event.

If a child could walk he was considered an adult within Jewish burial and mourning traditions. This is surprising, as the official age of reaching adulthood in Judaism is thirteen. But the rabbis had a good reason to use walking as a delineation: by this point in a child's life—close to age two—he had a full place in his family and community, and therefore his loss was felt as much as the loss of an adult.

The opposite of this can be seen in the funeral of a child who is less than a month old—only three people participate in such a funeral, two men and one woman.

A male infant who dies before he is circumcised is treated differently as well. Although the funeral is very much abbreviated, the child was nonetheless born to a Jewish family and must be buried in a Jewish cemetery as a full member of the Jewish community. Therefore a male infant who dies before he is circumcised (usually done on the eighth day of life) will be circumcised before he is buried and will be named then as well.[6]

This chapter has concentrated on the death practices and folk traditions of the Talmudic period rather than on its beliefs. Beliefs concerning afterlife and resurrection were integral to Judaism, even defining it in some senses. The possibilities of living in the "next world" and being resurrected in the time of the Messiah both compensated enormously for the difficulties and persecutions of life in Diaspora communities.

Both of these beliefs were established during the early Exilic period and did not change significantly afterward. While Jewish scholars argued about the details of afterlife and resurrection throughout the Middle Ages, they did not change their major philosophies surrounding those tenets. Not until very recently did attitudes concerning death begin to evolve within Judaism, and then only because they followed secular attitudes.

8

Jewish Death in the Modern World

Death practices among the Israelites remained almost identical from the Middle Bronze Age to the end of the biblical period, even though the people who practiced them identified with a variety of cultures and religions. Changes in death philosophies occurred only during the Exilic period, when the Jews were no longer tied to the land of the Bible. Talmudic death rituals and beliefs were only vaguely tied to those of the biblical period, loosely connected by prooftexts that served as justifications for already extant ceremonies.

From the Talmudic period onward there is enormous consistency in death practices yet again. Just as ancient practices survived for thousands of years despite periods of collapse and conquest, rabbinic death customs still survive within modern Judaism. In fact, only minor changes in death-related rituals took place between the Rabbinic period and the nineteenth century. In spite of the many periods of persecution and prosperity that the Jews experienced in those fifteen hundred years, death practices remained constant.

Then, suddenly, in the twentieth century, Jewish as well as Christian attitudes toward death and certain aspects of burial began to change again.

What makes our times so different from everything that came before, that even death practices, stable and static enough to survive major changes in religion and location, are now revolutionized? The modern period has produced new technologies that have had an impact not only on death but on the very process of dying. Sudden changes in the process of dying have affected Jewish as well as non-Jewish attitudes toward both dying and death.

Modern death customs are familiar to us, yet under scrutiny they will appear very foreign.[1] And though they are ultimately motivated by different concerns, our modern death practices still contain traces of the long familiar biblical ones.

Modern society is driven by technology, even where sickness, death, and dying are concerned. While today the majority of people, Jewish and non-Jewish, die in hospitals, in previous generations the majority of people died at home.[2] Since the advent of life-saving and life-extending medical technologies, not only have hospitals become the normal venue of dying and death but the very character of death itself has begun to change.

In the hospital, most family members request extraordinary measures to resuscitate their loved ones, even when there is no hope of extending life beyond a few more days, and even when there is no meaningful quality of life. The body can often be made to outlive the mind. In these increasingly common cases, we often talk about the lack of dignity afforded to the dying person. In the last decade the custom of writing a living will, a document that may provide specific instructions not to use extraordinary measures concerning one's own resuscitation, has taken root in American society as a sort of backlash against available technologies. Many Jews as well as non-Jews write living wills.

The Depersonalization and Denial of Death in Modern Society

When death finally occurs today, family members are not necessarily present. The patient is often alone in his hospital room, and a nurse is the first to discover the death.

The nurse will inform the attending physician. Only then will the next of kin be called, either by the doctor, the nurse, or by a hospital clergyman, meaning that a family member is only the second or third to know of the death, not the first.

By the time the next of kin arrives at the hospital, the staff will already have taken the body to the hospital morgue, generally located in the basement of the building. The removal of the body is designed to protect other patients and their visitors from the inevitability of death—people who are sick do not wish to be reminded that they too may die. Removing the body also protects family members from the physicality of death—the body is wheeled away within a closed gurney, generally one that resembles those used for laundry and linens, all common in hospital hallways. Death is all but invisible.

In some cases a rabbi serving as hospital chaplain may accompany the body and stay with it in the hospital morgue, but more often than not the integral Jewish tradition of guarding the body is simply abandoned.

After being informed of the death, the family generally contacts a funeral home. From this point forward (and an argument can be made for earlier as well), everyone speaks in euphemisms. We do not say "mortician" but "funeral director," not "coffin" but "casket," not "mortuary" but "funeral parlor," as if it were someone's living room. And we say that the patient has "passed away" or "gone to a better place," rather than starkly acknowledging that he died.

All this is ostensibly to preserve the dignity of the individual after death, but more practically it helps to shield the survivors for the actuality of their loss. The expression we hear least in our culture is a simple "he died." The term "death" evokes permanence instead of, for instance, passing to a better place, where you can in theory return from, or at least be joined at.

Once the family has chosen a funeral home (either through tactful recommendation or from the Yellow Pages), their job is finished. The funeral home will pick up the body from the hospital (often in an unobtrusive station wagon rather than a hearse) and bring it back for embalming. When the spouse or child of the deceased comes to the funeral home to meet with the director and make some decisions, the body is not seen. In fact it is not seen again until the funeral itself, if at all.

The family now selects a coffin. Coffins are enormously expensive, but the consumer is forced to buy one, no matter what the price. Even the plain pine coffins used for Jewish burials cost more than a thousand dollars.

In Western culture most coffins (caskets) are lined with satin and include pillows or cushions. Presumably this is to make the deceased look comfortable or, more precisely, to make him look like he is merely comfortably sleeping, not dead. This is another way that our society disguises and avoids the physicality of death.

Once the coffin has been selected, the staff of the funeral home prepares the body in a back room. This preparation almost always includes embalming. Embalming and the use of cosmetics on the corpse are done to preserve the corpse in the most lifelike condition until the burial; they are all denials of death.[3]

Contrary to popular belief, no law requires embalming or even coffins in America. Jews in America today who know this do not have their dead embalmed; others, not knowing the law, do.

The Burial and Its Rituals

Once the preparations for the funeral (including the preparing of the body) are complete, little else happens before the funeral itself. One of the few things that separate Jewish funerals today from non-Jewish ones is that non-Jewish families often choose to have a wake and a viewing, laying out the body in the funeral parlor (or in a home of a relative or the home of the deceased himself) for a set number of days until the funeral. By contrast, Jewish funerals and burials are still held within a day of the death, according to ancient tradition.

Both Jewish and non-Jewish funeral ceremonies include eulogies by relatives as well as by clergymen. Jews may also recite the traditional hymns and the Mourners' Kaddish during the funeral ceremony.

Following the funeral ceremony, some, but not all, of the funeral party goes on to the cemetery. Modern cemeteries may be located far from the site of death and even miles from the site of the funeral. Jews are traditionally buried in specific Jewish cemeteries, or at the very least in a marked-off section of a town's Christian cemetery.

The body travels to the cemetery in a hearse. Cars follow one another, driving slowly, with their headlights on, an informal but well-accepted sign of a funeral procession. In Jewish funerals, the funerary procession of Talmudic (and even biblical) times still takes place but in an abbreviated form—only from the place where the hearse parks to the grave that is no more than several yards away.

The burial itself exemplifies how uncomfortable modern society is about the physicality of death. Instead of a family member digging the actual grave, cemetery workers dig it in advance, most often with machinery. In most cases the grave is invisible, covered by a grasslike rug in an attempt to disguise the finality of burial until and often beyond the last possible second. This is also the case in Jewish burials.

After the coffin is in the ground, family members disperse, leaving the cemetery workers to close the grave over the coffin.

This is considered the most emotionally painful part of the ceremony because of its finality, yet family members rarely participate in it today.

Even in Jewish funerals, where closing the grave is legally the responsibility of the children of the deceased, the family members each contribute only one symbolic shovelful and then let the cemetery workers finish the job.

A number of Jewish customs that are recent innovations also reflect this modern denial of death. Jews today use only the back of the shovel to fill in the grave, in order to differentiate this use of such a common tool from its regular use. Modern Jews also put the shovel into the earth for the next person to pick up, rather than handing it directly from person to person. This is done so that the "contagion" of death will leave the mourners alone.[4]

Both these customs are rooted in superstition, and both show the relatively recent denial of death that Judaism shares with the rest of modern society.

Ancient versus Modern

Even while the Jewish ceremonies are carried out, even while mourners recite the Kaddish and tear their clothes, modern Jews share with the rest of modern society the fear of the actuality and physicality of death. This fear is diametrically opposed to the biblical and rabbinic approaches, and reflects the changes in attitudes toward death brought about by our modern technological society. Technology has made death seem bad instead of inevitable. Because we can cure the sick, we attempt to do it to the limit, putting off death as long as possible, perhaps longer than it should be put off. Modern technologies have made the process more fearful rather than less. They have taken respect away from the dying.

This is very different from the respect accorded to dead elders in the biblical world, where the tombs of family members were placed in open fields so that they could stand guard over family property. A man who dies naturally at home, when his time has come, retains respect. A man who dies unnaturally, fighting death every step of the way, loses something in the process.

Not everything about Jewish death has changed. In the world of premodern Judaism, death was a state that brought the person closer to God and to heaven. From the biblical world at least through the Middle Ages, a dying man would be expected to give his blessing to his children, and other family members would ask him for forgiveness, presumably so that he would not remain angry at them in the realm of God. This is still within our current mind-set—we want to make peace with people before their death, and if we do not, we regret it afterward. The custom of asking the dead for forgiveness goes back to the Bible—one of the powers of the dead was that of vengeance, and if a man forgave you before his death, he would not need to take vengeance on you afterward.

Backlash and Reaction to Modern Attitudes Toward Death

By the middle of the twentieth century the disrespectful nature of hospital death was recognized by religious groups, though not by Jews until more recently. The pendulum is swinging back again, in several different ways.

The reaction against life-sustaining and life-prolonging technology comes in the form of the hospice movement. The intentions of this movement are to make the last days or weeks of a dying person's life as comfortable and fulfilled as possible. Hospice rejects the concept of taking extraordinary measures to save the life of a patient who will soon die anyway, and it avoids the use of medical technology (beyond that of pain relief and symptom treatment) to prolong the life of a fatally ill person who is suffering. Instead, hospice is concerned with the soul of the terminally ill patient. The goal of the hospice movement is to offer death with dignity, at home, and with one's family nearby.

The hospice movement unconsciously reflects the premodern death philosophy. Hospice patients and their families focus on the upcoming death without denial, much as people did before the modern era.

A second backlash against modern attitudes about death is religious in nature. While it does not come from organized religion, it is nonetheless deeply tied to the death beliefs of both Judaism and Christianity.

Belief in an afterlife is becoming more acceptable than it has been in recent times. But in today's scientifically based society, it is no longer based on blind faith. Instead, people claim to have had near-death experiences, visions that take place during moments in which they are clinically dead. They interpret these visions as hints of the afterlife.

Near-death experiences are often strikingly alike. According to most descriptions, a person experiences a distance from his body, in some cases even floats above it. Next he either walks or floats through a long tunnel. At the end of the tunnel is a strong white light, or brightness, that acts as a powerful beacon. At this point the person experiences great feelings of joy or peace. Many near-death experiences end there, but some continue with the person entering the light and even seeing long-deceased family members on the other side.

In the last decade scientists have been researching these near-death experiences and have been able to explain most of their phenomena in terms of biology and physiology. But the survivors of these experiences interpret their physiological responses and visions in terms of their own cultural and religious biases. They imagine that they have approached the light of a Judeo-Christian heaven.

This heaven is seldom concrete—people see lightness and experience feelings of comfort or peace, but generally do not see specific angels with harps or Saint Peter opening specific, physical gates. This is because most people today, regardless of their official religion, have only an indirect, vague idea of the biblical and postbiblical realities of heaven. Most people's religious education stops short of investigating death beliefs, which is why most of us cling to vague associations among heaven, godliness, and light. People who have had near-death experiences draw upon these loose associations for their interpretations.

Interestingly, almost no one who has had near-death experiences interprets the light as the fires of hell. This is in line with data gathered in two separate 1997 surveys.[5] According to the surveys, 90 percent of Americans believe in heaven but only 73 percent believe in hell. That means that at least 17 percent of people believe in heaven but not hell.

There is more—94 percent of Americans think they will go to heaven when they die while only 6 percent think they will go to hell. These numbers mean that in the face of death, people want to believe in heaven in the most general terms. They do not want to believe in hell.

The results of these polls also mean that people are returning to religion as a way of reconciling themselves with death, as the excitement of life-extending technology morphs into acceptance of its limitations. The farther away from biblical culture and beliefs we move as a society, the stronger the pull to return to them becomes, at least when we are faced with death.

Jewish death in the modern world looks very similar to all other modern deaths—the rabbinic traditions to which Jews adhere are only additions to secularized ceremonies and thought processes. But shouldn't the ancient death practices of Judaism show up more visibly on the modern landscape of death? They should and do. But modern death-related attitudes and ceremonies are not the right places to look.

9

A History of Mortuary Theory

Compared with the large body of anthropological literature that is concerned with mortuary theory, the few dozen books and articles on death in the biblical world look like a paltry set indeed.

Death has been analyzed statistically, it has been quantified and qualified, it has been philosophized, and it has been examined from postmodern perspectives. Yet death in the biblical world does not figure into any of these studies. When a scholar makes a specific study of death in Iron Age Israel (or Bronze Age Israel, or Persian period Israel), he is generally unable to incorporate much of earlier mortuary scholarship into his own work.

Nineteenth-Century Theories of Death

The earliest mortuary theory was not recognized as such at the time. It was part and parcel of nineteenth-century "proto"-

anthropology. Nineteenth-century anthropological studies recorded the existence of funerals and burials as part of larger cultural studies. The best known of these were studies by E. B. Tylor and James Frazer.

The nineteenth-century interest in death practices focused on "primitive" beliefs about the afterlife. These early anthropologists encountered ancestor worship in the societies they observed and viewed it as an inferior first step to modern beliefs and practices concerning the dead. This approach is sometimes called the evolutionary school of thought, since it assumes that modern ideas evolved out of those still held by more traditional societies.

Modern scholars who deal in mortuary issues seldom give serious consideration to these nineteenth-century beginnings. This is true both within and outside biblical studies.

The Early Twentieth Century: Early Sociological Anthropology

The next stage of mortuary theory dates to the early years of the twentieth century and has a sociological bent. This school is associated with two men, Robert Hertz and Arnold van Gennep, who came to the same conclusions based on completely separate data, and by coincidence published within a year of each other.

Both men found that many societies do not view death as a one-time, instantaneous event but as a process.[1]

Hertz looked at secondary burial on Borneo, where people believed that the soul did not die when the body of an individual died. Instead the soul went into a sort of limbo, no longer residing with the living but not yet with the souls of the dead either. Because of this belief, they held only a preliminary funeral ceremony at the time of death. The main funeral came later.

Only when the decay was complete and the bones had dried did the soul leave the body and join the community of the dead. This joining of the dead—not the physical death of the body—was cause for a funeral feast. On Borneo, death was a process in three distinct stages—physical death, decay, and dry bones. The funeral ceremonies reflected each of these stages.

Several examples of secondary burial are evident in the biblical world, from the plastered skulls of Neolithic Jericho to both the Chalcolithic and Roman-period ossuaries. Yet in almost no instances do modern scholars rely on this early school of thought for information about secondary burials. One reason is that in most periods, Canaanite society was illiterate. Because no texts discuss the beliefs behind secondary burial, it is considered better not to speculate at all, and certainly not prudent to base speculations on research from faraway unrelated cultures.

The same holds true for secondary burial in the Roman period. Although there are many examples of Jewish ossuaries, the Talmud is silent on disinterment and re-placement of bones in such containers. The idea of death as a process may indeed be at work here, but again there is no proof for this.

In spite of the interesting explanations this theoretical school of thought offers for death in the biblical world and in early Judaism, there is understandable scholarly resistance to taking these ideas out of their original contexts. But the scholarship is inconsistent—this reluctance to extrapolate from external theories is replaced with inappropriate applications of external theories.

Functionalism and Structuralism

The next significant development for mortuary theory—functionalism—took place in the 1950s and early 1960s. There are two schools of thought within functionalism, the first of which states that every ritual action has a direct function within the society as a whole. Thus weeping over a corpse is done not merely out of grief or sadness; rather, weeping functions as an affirmation of the continued social ties between the group and the dead individual.

The second school of functionalism is chiefly associated with B. Malinowski. His somewhat more radical approach stated that all human customs ultimately derive from the physical needs of the body. Ceremonies surrounding death are a function of the organic processes of the survivors.

Functionalism was a construct not only for an explanation of death customs, though they have been fit into its mold. Nor does functionalism help in analyzing the archaeological or textual sources of the biblical world. While funeral ceremonies of the biblical world clearly had personal as well as societal functions, it is impossible to guess what they might mean in the abstract.

Structuralism, a school of thought that developed out of functionalism, is somewhat more useful for analyzing the biblical world. Structuralism states that there is a natural logic and order to the subconscious which is reflected in outward cultural expressions or symbols, including language, myth, art, social relationships, and social organization. Thus if there is a dual structure to a society, as there was in Claude Lévi-Strauss's example of the Bororo of South America, one should see dualities everywhere—from social structure made up of two clans, to two heroes in mythology.

While structuralism, like functionalism, did not develop in specific response to mortuary data, it can be viably applied to it. For instance, in the biblical world the physical structures of the tombs of the Canaanites and the Israelites mimicked domestic house structures. The idea of living space is part of the society of the living and is also part of the society of the dead. Here, finally, is a theory that has been successfully translated to the mortuary archaeology of the biblical world.

Statistical Analyses of Mortuary Practices and Their Uses in the Biblical World

The 1960s and early 1970s saw the development of processual archaeology, or the "New Archaeology." This movement affected mortuary archaeology more deeply than any school of thought discussed so far, but barely made an impact on the mortuary archaeology of ancient Israel.

The premise of the New Archaeology was to introduce scientific methodologies into archaeology and anthropology. Anthropology is traditionally considered a social science; the proponents of the New Archaeology hoped that more scientific methodologies would help lift anthropology to the level of the hard sciences.

One of the main philosophies of the New Archaeology was systems theory, an idea borrowed from biology. Systems theory states that all systems within an organism are related to one another and depend on one another. In the human example it means that the pulmonary system is tied to the circulatory system, the cardiovascular system, and the respiratory system.

When translated into the terms of anthropology, systems theory states that all systems of a society are related to one another and depend on one another. The hierarchical system of any given culture is tied to, among other things, its language, its mythologies, and the ceremonies that surround its life-cycle events (including mortuary customs).

The other aspect of the New Archaeology was "hypothetical-deductive" reasoning. This meant that a researcher must begin with a hypothesis rather than with straight data. Only after he formulated his hypothesis could he look at the data as a way of testing that hypothesis. If the hypothesis did not stand up to the data, the researcher might then revise his hypothesis.

Lewis Binford, one of several key anthropologists who promoted the New Archaeology, wrote a number of widely read articles on mortuary practices from the standpoint of the New Archaeology. One, published in 1971, is still considered the gold standard by most people working in mortuary theory, no matter what part of the world their data come from. This article puts forward a deceptively simple premise, that mortuary variability—the idea that a society uses more than one type of burial—is associated with hierarchical social complexity.[2]

In simpler language, Binford was saying that if a society has more than one way of burying its dead, that same society will almost certainly have an upper class and a lower class, rulers and peasants, and so forth. This class-based view of mortuary practices further implies that the upper classes will bury their dead in one way while the lower classes will bury their dead in another way. Someone important who dies will be given an elaborate burial treatment that might even disrupt town life for several days. Someone unimportant will be given the simplest, quickest, least disruptive burial treatment available.[3]

Binford tested his hypothesis against a number of societies, the least complex of which was a hunter-gatherer society, and the most complex of which was a settled, agricultural community. He examined several categories of burial treatment in each society to reach his conclusions.

Just as he expected, Binford found that the settled agriculturalists did in fact have significantly more mortuary variability than the other societies, while the hunter-gatherers had variability based only on the most basic differences, such as age and gender.

But Binford's work presented some problems. The main one was that the group he used as examples provided more than the usual amount of information. He was not dealing with societies that were known only from their material remains, mythologies, or religious texts. He was dealing with societies that yielded all these sources and more. In the case of the groups he had chosen, he would definitely know if his conclusions were right or wrong.

This is not the case in the real world of ancient mortuary practices. Almost never is all the information available. One of the pitfalls of mortuary archaeology is that, since Binford, the remains of tombs have often been used to determine how complex a society was. This is a backward approach, since Binford's correlation between mortuary variability and complexity does not take into account several other factors.

What if, instead of building large and elaborate tombs for its most important members, a society buried them in the old tombs of their ancestors as a sign of respect? This was done in the biblical world. To an archaeologist armed with Binford's theory, it might look like the most special members of biblical society were not getting any special treatment at all. Our biblical "gathering to ancestors" does not fit into this scheme.

Or what if even the poorest stratum of a society saved its wealth and spent it all on elaborate burials? These burials might easily be archaeologically mistaken for burials of wealthy individuals.

Lastly, what if a society had horizontal stratification, rather than vertical stratification—what if there were several different clans that lived in the same region, but each buried their dead in a different manner? Following Binford's hypothesis, these differences might be mistaken for different levels in a class structure rather than recognized as groups of people of equal rank from various clans.

Israel in the biblical period was a society that used several different types of burials—within cities, under the floors of houses, and outside of cities, in separate cemeteries. Different treatments for bodies included burying the dead in several positions (extended, flexed, and semi-flexed) and practicing secondary burial.

Following Binford's approach, the diversity of this data shows that biblical society was in fact a complex, stratified society. But we cannot interpret beyond this, as Binford claims one should always be able to do with such data.

In the biblical world it is difficult to say which burials were of individuals of higher or lower status. Perhaps being buried outside the city was considered only a small disruption of the city routine and was therefore used for lower-status individuals. Or perhaps the labor that was necessary to cut acrosolia tombs made such burials a large disruption to the routine of a city. In that case such burials might have been a mark of respect reserved for high-status individuals.

Perhaps such distinctions had to do with clans or with the remnants of ancient tribal distinctions rather than with a class system of stratification. The same questions could be raised for other types of burial, such as masonry-constructed tombs beneath houses, and shaft-and-chamber tombs cut into the slopes of a city's defense system. Because there are so few discernible patterns, and since both rich and poor assemblages of tomb contents are found in all types of tombs in all locations, there is no way to know which of these theories might be correct.

The New Archaeology included a heavy emphasis on statistics, and Binford's classifications were only the beginning.

Other scholars, such as J. Tainter, have analyzed a variety of statistical methodologies in order to determine how well each might work for mortuary archaeology, eventually concluding that some of these techniques were more applicable than others.[4]

Tainter also stated something very important for the biblical world, something that is seldom discussed. He pointed out that a main problem with all such statistical approaches is that they must have consistent databases to work well. The lack of consistent databases is one of the main reasons why most analytical techniques do not work well for the mortuary data of the biblical world. The data, while certainly diverse, are often incomplete.

Beyond this, mathematical approaches to mortuary data cannot take into account tomb reuse. Not only is little energy needed to reuse an old tomb (entailing only slight disruption of social life), reused tombs can be a mark of either insignificance or significance, something that cannot be quantified appropriately.

Post-Processual Archaeology

Following the New Archaeology (or processual archaeology) came the post-processualists of the late 1980s and early 1990s, a school of theorists who objected to the New Archaeology for reasons much like those stated above.

For instance, post-processualists believe that the mathematical techniques that are still so popular actually inhibit researchers from approaching the data objectively. They also argue that such techniques downgrade the human element as irrational and neglect the material in favor of methodology.

This viewpoint is the most helpful for the type of mortuary data available from the biblical world. It acknowledges that although the mortuary data from the biblical world does not always stand up to statistical analyses, it remains valid and important.

There have been several attempts to apply statistical analyses to the tombs of the biblical world, though none of these studies has used Iron Age materials. At least three such studies exist, two of which deal with the Intermediate Bronze Age and one with the Middle Bronze Age. All three studies used mortuary materials from the Jericho cemetery, but the two on the Intermediate Bronze Age reached opposing conclusions.[5]

How is it possible for the very same data to yield contradictory conclusions? There are two reasons. First, the researchers used different statistical techniques to manipulate the same data, ending up with different results. Second, the cemetery at Jericho was originally excavated by Kathleen Kenyon in the 1950s, when modern excavation and related research techniques were brand new. One researcher trusted Kenyon's data and used it as is, while the other did not.

Intent, Tombs, and the Biblical World

While some of the major developments within mortuary studies can be successfully applied to the mortuary data from the biblical world, most cannot. It appears that the material from ancient Israel is different from that of the rest of the world. Because established theories and statistics cannot be successfully applied to biblical data, researchers can more freely explore the idea of intent. Mortuary materials show the conscious intentions of the society at hand, as opposed to the unconscious ones.

Unconscious intentions abound in the remains of domestic areas. How a household was set up, what it contained, and its pattern of use are issues of unconscious intent. No one intended the remains of a household to be found later on, and no one carefully planned the condition of such remains for posterity.

The same is true for temples, palaces, and other public structures. Like domestic structures, these public buildings show only unconscious intentions. While their size and excess may serve as symbols of the wealth and social organization of the people who built them, they were built to be used, not to remain for posterity.

By contrast, tombs were intended to remain in place permanently. A tomb is an advertisement for a society. Here is a modern analogy: When a person wants to buy a car, he will try to find out how well the engine runs, what the company's track record is, and what the car's price is relative to other cars of the same type. He might go to *Consumer Reports* or a similar publication for that sort of information.

But a consumer magazine will not tell someone what image the company hopes to project. In order to find out the product's image, the buyer must turn to the company's own advertisements. They might include an image of a beautiful woman sitting on a car's hood, or a muscular man in sunglasses behind its wheel. The message of the advertisement is clear: Buy this car and you will be handsome and/or attract beautiful women.

The message of the tomb is just as clear. Tombs say things such as: We are a society of warriors. The tombs of Middle Bronze Age Canaan say this by containing a disproportionate number of weapons. As Canaanite society was barely coming out of its period of collapse, being a warrior was a societal priority, which is why many people were portrayed as warriors after death.

Alternately a tomb might say: Even though historical texts might hide it, we are a wealthy society, with a powerful elite class. The tombs of Late Bronze Age Canaan said exactly this, as some of them had a disproportionate number of riches and were built on an unusually large scale. The Canaanites were ruled by the Egyptians in the Late Bronze Age, yet at least one stratum of their society proclaimed its wealth and power for posterity.

Not all tomb objects demonstrate intent. Certainly provisions for food and items of personal adornment do, but other categories of items are left in the tomb by coincidence or by accident such as a button or toggle pin that held clothing on the corpse.[6] The intention was to dress the corpse; the button that remains in the archaeological record remains only coincidentally. An example of an item left in a tomb by accident is a knife point, or arrowhead, still between the ribs of the skeleton. The weapon that killed the person and could not be extracted from his body remains in the tomb only by accident. Both coincidental and accidental tomb items are special "extras" for archaeologists, giving a bit of nonintentional information about the individual buried in a mainly intentional context.

Thinking about intention is perhaps the only theoretical approach to mortuary studies that takes into account the nature of the remains of the biblical world, rather than borrowing and applying other theoretical approaches.

Still, a question remains. Some statistical methodologies do not work well for the tombs of the biblical world, since the databases from the tombs of Canaan and Israel are not large enough. Why does this region, a region with such interesting mortuary remains, not have materials that are adequate for analysis?

10

The Politics of Death in Israel

The director of an excavation gathers his senior staff around him at the end of an excavation day. Just that morning the team has found a human burial from the Late Bronze Age, a simple one with only a few offerings. The team has worked hard throughout the day, excavating with toothpicks and nail brushes, careful not to damage the fragile bones.

But there is a problem: the day is over and still the skeleton is not ready to be removed from the ground. Put a tarp over it, the director instructs, then dump dirt over the tarp. Never mind if some spills back into the burial, making more work for tomorrow, just make sure that skeleton is completely covered so that no one can know it is there.

And, he goes on, do not refer to this burial by name. Use a code word when you talk about it. You never can tell how word gets around.

Why take such precautions? He is afraid of roaming inspectors loosely associated with, or unofficially reporting to, the

Ministry of Religious Affairs, a branch of the Israeli government. These inspectors specifically look for human bones. If they find any, they confiscate them and work toward shutting down the excavation.

Religion versus Archaeology in Israel

Israel is a democratic state with a national religion, Judaism. Israel's government therefore includes Jewish religious parties, which have at heart the concerns of the country's Ultra-Orthodox minority. These religious parties have always had a say in the democratic process. In recent years their influence has increased enormously, especially where archaeology is concerned.

Since the founding of the State of Israel, Israeli nationalism has in part expressed itself through national archaeology. The site of Masada is an important tourist attraction, as are several spots within Jerusalem. Through archaeology, Israel is able to proclaim the Jews' national identification with the ancient land of Israel.

Forming a national identity through identification with the past was not an issue until recently—it was simply an accepted, harmless part of the Israeli mind-set. This changed following the 1967 Six Day War. The Israelis ended this war with more territory than they had had before it—they now had access to East and West Jerusalem, not just West Jerusalem.

Control over East Jerusalem was very important from religious as well as political perspectives. East Jerusalem was the site of the ancient Temple Mount, where both the First and Second Temples are supposed to have been located.[1] Archaeologists too were excited about East Jerusalem. They could now excavate the City of David, an area of significance to anyone interested in the Bible.

This is why archaeological activity intensified in Jerusalem in the late 1960s and early 1970s. Although British, Jewish, and Arab archaeologists had been excavating this ancient city since the late nineteenth century, now was a time of greater movement. The intensification of work was precisely why the controversy, brewing quietly since the beginnings of the modern state, exploded.

With archaeology more visible, the digging up of human bones also became more visible. Ultra-Orthodox groups began to protest, harassing archaeologists, and picketing in front of excavation sites. The Ultra-Orthodox believe that any human burial found in the land of Israel may be a Jewish burial. Although they admit that the Jews are not the only group to have lived (and died) in Israel, they prefer to err on the side of caution. And, their argument goes on, exhuming a Jewish grave is against the Jewish religion. Not only is it disrespectful to the dead, it is a blasphemous act.

These religious groups allow for the reburial of Jewish remains only in very specific circumstances, for instance if the placement of one grave is damaging to another. They often dismiss some of the other allowances for disinterment and reburial made by the Talmud. They find exhumation for any reason, but especially during the course of building construction or archaeological excavations, humiliating to the dead. They argue that the dead feel fear when they are moved, because they think they are being brought before God for judgment. They also sometimes argue that moving the bones of a Jewish person will damage his completeness (even though the flesh has already long decayed), which in turn will prevent him from being resurrected in the time of the Messiah.

The arguments of the Ultra-Orthodox groups do not take into account the long-lived traditions of moving the bones of the dead, as well as secondary burial, within Israelite and Jewish history. Both archaeology and biblical texts offer evidence that the Israelites regularly "gathered" the bones of their dead "to their ancestors," reopening family tombs, placing the newly dead inside, then replacing the capping stones. Jewish ossuaries from the first century offer clear instances of exhumation from the early Talmudic period. Those who protest archaeological excavation and call for the reburial of excavated human remains of Jews do not acknowledge any of these older traditions.

Even according to normative Modern Orthodoxy (as opposed to Ultra-Orthodoxy), disinterment and reburial violate *kibud hamet,* the honor accorded to the dead. This has been stated by such mainstream scholars as Maurice Lamm, long before the issues between archaeology and religion reached the public eye.

The belief that the dead should never again be touched after burial, a purely modern manifestation, is a long way from the original intentions of early Judaism but is nonetheless fashioned from the older traditions. These include the traditions of burial within a day following death (from the Bible), and that of purifying and caring for the body immediately after death (from the Talmud). These older traditions have been conflated with modern squeamishness about the physicality of death and reinterpreted to mean that the dead should never again be touched once they are buried.

The rabbinate had discussed the exhumation and reburial of Jewish remains on a case-by-case basis since at least World War I, when the families of war dead wanted proper burial of their loved ones near their homes. But exhumation and reburial became a true issue in Israel only after the 1967 Six Day War. Protests escalated from that point. In at least one documented instance, protesters even objected to the excavation of animal bones, mistaking them for human.

During the 1980s and 1990s the issues spread out from Jerusalem to archaeology in the rest of the country. Controversy culminated in 1994, when Israel's attorney general was forced to reconsider an earlier ruling, eventually concluding that human remains found in archaeological contexts were not, in fact, archaeological artifacts, and that control of such remains at any excavation site should be given to the Ministry of Religious Affairs. The remains were to be reburied immediately in a religious ceremony.

The ruling was a landmark. Religious reburial of human remains was now firmly institutionalized. During 1996 more than three hundred boxes of human remains, of Jews and non-Jews alike, were delivered from archaeological contexts and warehouses to the Ministry of Religious Affairs for reburial.

Also in 1996 the Ultra-Orthodox deputy housing minister closed several archaeological excavations simply because of a concern that human remains might be found, not because of any specific remains. By 1998 the laws had changed in favor of these groups. Representatives of the Ministry of Religious Affairs are now required to be present at certain excavations. In a number of instances, these representatives have actually removed bones from archaeological contexts without supervision. In deference to the religiously motivated political parties, the Israeli government is considering the appointment of rabbinical representatives to the Archaeological Council, to ensure the representation of religious interests. At this writing such appointments have not yet been made but are likely to emerge in the near future.

Archaeologists find many burials on the tops of tells. High spots like these have traditionally been used by Bedouin groups over the last several hundred years. The bodies invariably point east, or southeast, toward Mecca, in traditional Muslim style. Depending on their contexts, however, these burials may nonetheless be confiscated by the Religious Authority. Burials from the Iron Age may also be confiscated, though Canaanites, Philistines, and foreigners lived and were buried in the land of Israel in that period alongside the Israelites.[2]

As a result of these claims, the skeletal remains of premodern Jews and even ancient Israelites (as well as the skeletal remains of a certain number of non-Jews) have been posthumously adopted into the modern Jewish community, given modern religious Jewish funerals long after their deaths.

These issues, troubling as they are, are not unique to Israel. The same debate is currently going on in America concerning a nine-thousand-year-old skeleton found in Kennewick, Washington. The skeleton is significant for understanding how the first Homo sapiens came to the Americas, and, with the right scientific analysis, would be able to tell us a lot about those first people. But this skeleton is being claimed by several tribes of Native Americans who say it is their ancestor. In spite of flaws in the tribes' arguments, such as the fact that Kennewick Man predates their existence by several thousand years, and the fact that their territory did not originally include the area where they now live and where Kennewick Man was found, the U.S. Army Corps of Engineers has decided to give the skeleton to the tribes so that they can rebury it in a religious ceremony. The skeleton was subject to only limited scientific analysis, and even though several scholars are suing for the right to study the bones anthropologically, it is likely that Kennewick Man will be returned to the ground unexamined.

Ancient Burials and Modern Sensibilities

What is it like to dig up a human burial? That depends in large part on the age of the burial. I have excavated Bedouin burials in Israel, ones that were interred less than a century ago, and have also excavated ancient burials in Israel from the Bronze and Iron Ages.

It is easy to tell an ancient burial from a more recent one, and all in all, excavating ancient human remains feels much the same as excavating artifacts. Proper analysis can yield all sorts of information about diet and physical condition, which can then translate into sociocultural information.

But there is something distinctly unpleasant about digging up more recent burials. To begin with, recent burials are often complete—the only missing bones might be the smallest finger and toe joints. These small bones are easily carried off by rodents and large insects, but the rest of the skeleton is generally intact.

Recent burials are distinctive in a number of other ways that even lay people can recognize. The bone, for instance, is often whiter than ancient bone. But most distinctively, there is often a very faint, almost imperceptible odor to recent burials, just enough to remind you that what you are excavating is organic, not static rock or brick, that it was once a living, breathing person, and that the processes of decomposition that brought it to its current, skeletal state are not quite finished.

This stark reminder of the humanness of a burial leads easily to flights of imagination: how the person must have looked at burial, laid out on his back, hair up or down, fancy or plain clothing. The reality of the skeleton as a human is all too clear.

The most disturbing thing of all when dealing with a recent burial, one made within a century, is that the family of the individual may still live in the immediate area. This is certainly a possibility when Bedouin remains are found on the top of high archaeological tells. In these situations it is even possible to speculate that the Arab guard hired to protect the excavation from looters is a descendant of the person whose remains are being excavated on the site.

On this basis there is good reason to object to excavating human burials. When a death is so recent, within fifty or one hundred years, the bones do not seem like archaeological artifacts; they still retain the identity of the individual and of the group that buried him. These are the reasons that, in the last decade, archaeologists have stopped excavating such burials as artifacts and instead remove them intact and rebury them to the side of their work areas.

But sensitivity to Bedouin families and religious practices have little to do with the Ultra-Orthodox objections to excavating human burials that were outlined above. The debate between religion and science will not be put to rest for a long time.

The Problem of Tomb Looting in Israel

Neither skeletal remains nor the remains of artifacts from tombs in Israel can be formed into sufficient databases. Since the religious reburial of unexamined human remains is growing in Israel, it becomes more difficult than ever to complete a database—how can archaeologists classify the total number of skeletons, record how many are male or female, adult or subadult, how many died of disease, how many of natural causes, and how many by violence, when every skeleton is whisked away before a physical anthropologist can look at it?

And when burials are yanked out by religious inspectors for reburial, without archaeological supervision or methodology, it is impossible to see their contexts, to record how many and which artifacts were placed with the bodies, and in what part of the tomb they were placed. Without proper excavation, it is sometimes impossible to record accurately even the shape of the tomb.

And there are other current problems besides this most serious one of religious interference with archaeology. First, much of the mortuary material from Israel was excavated before modern methods were commonly used. Such methods were introduced in the 1950s, yet many sites in Israel were excavated in the 1920s, 1930s, and 1940s. Some sites have excavation histories that go back as far as the late nineteenth century. In premodern excavations, not everything was saved or recorded. Sometimes the bones were disposed of, sometimes the excavators paid no attention to walls that divide tombs and separate different interments in the same tomb, and sometimes the pottery and less interesting objects were neglected. Citations in older excavation reports might mention "several beads" or "scarabs" or "juglets," and since photographs and drawings were executed inconsistently, the modern researcher is often left with gaping holes in the data.

Another reason for holes in the data has to do with tomb robbery and the antiquities trade. Israel is the only country in the Middle East in which antiquities dealing is still legal. All other countries in the region (including those with difficult political histories such as Iraq) have made the buying and selling of antiquities illegal, as a way of stopping the looting of ancient sites.

Israel has some laws regulating the sale of antiquities. One states that no recently found objects may be sold, only those found years ago, before the laws were in place. But it is nearly impossible to prove when an object was discovered. Even though each piece of merchandise owned by an antiquities dealer has its own registration number, old registration numbers are easily reassigned to newly acquired antiquities.

When a site is looted by antiquities robbers, its artifacts are ripped out of their contexts. Without a clear context, an artifact is all but useless from a scholarly point of view. There is much more to an artifact than its aesthetic or intrinsic value. Archaeologists need to know if a ceramic jug, for instance, came from a domestic area or not. And if it came from a domestic area, was it in a kitchen or a courtyard or a tomb under a house? Was it in a bedroom or a lavatory? How people used their artifacts tells us much more about their society than the artifacts themselves, devoid of context.

Not only is the context removed from the artifact when it is stolen, the context itself is often ruined for scholars as well. When robbers loot a site, they commonly dig trenches through its center or its sides, destroying architecture such as walls, floors, and delicate collapsed sections of roofing as they go. If the looting is particularly thorough, an archaeologist coming to the site later will even find it difficult to tell what sort of building the structure was. If it was a temple, and the looters uprooted an altar, archaeologists may never recognize that it was a temple, or may reconstruct the altar in a mistaken place.

The problem of looting is particularly intense when it comes to ancient tombs as opposed to settlement sites. First, tombs are often the only source of unbroken, undamaged ceramics, and are also a particularly good source of objets d'art, gold and silver jewelry, and other precious objects. These items bring more money on the open market than do broken shards, and the tomb robbers, often poor peasants who engage in tomb robbing to feed their families, know that the middlemen they sell to are happiest with intact pieces.

The second reason is that once a tomb is uncovered by a tomb robber, he knows that it is likely to be part of a larger cemetery. Other tombs will be actively sought in the vicinity, and almost always found, when money is at stake.

What can be done? Rather than expending political energy on the religious reburial of ancient human remains, Israel could instead work on strengthening its laws against antiquities selling. If there were no legal market, if casual tourists no longer thought that bringing home a juglet or a Roman coin were possibilities, demand would fall. Once that happened, suppliers would begin looking for other sources of income. While the antiquities trade would almost certainly go underground—rather than disappear—if made illegal, even that would lessen its impact on archaeology.

For the moment, the twin issues of modern religious objections to archaeology and modern tomb-looting are both unavoidable problems for the archaeology of death in ancient Israel. Ironically, both issues offer cultural evidence useful to archaeologists.

Tomb robbing, while today seen as a problem that hinders

scientific study, is an ancient profession. Tomb robbers have been active in Israel (as well as in Egypt, Syria, and Mesopotamia) since antiquity. Not everyone feared the wrath of the ancestors. Besides, the prizes—the gold and silver jewelry, the precious artifacts and amulets—were well worth the risk. Today's tomb robbers are in essence continuing one of the longest-lived burial traditions of them all—and they are doing it for the same reasons that people did it in antiquity—the need for money. This continuity of tradition, though illegal and harmful from a scientific position, attests to the fact that local people, those who live among the cemeteries, have been reacting to them and treating them in the same way for millennia.

Similarly the Ultra-Orthodox protests over the excavation of tombs has a long history, in spite of the fact that these religious protesters have forgotten that ancient Jewish bodies were often touched after burial. By arguing that all Jewish burials found in archaeological contexts must be reburied with a religious ceremony, the Ultra-Orthodox are creating their own modern identities as the descendants of generations of Jews and Israelites who have lived in the land of Israel. In doing so they are mimicking what the Israelites and Canaanites did thousands of years earlier. Just as the Israelites formed their group identity through burial in family tombs, and claimed their land—and their identities as landowners—through family tombs, these modern Jews form identities through similar claims. They claim descent from and connections to their biblical "ancestors" through the reburial controversy.

In both the ancient and modern cases, whether or not the claim is true—whether the Israelites owned the land prior to the burial, and whether the modern Jews are direct descendants of the Israelites—is all but irrelevant. Just as tomb looting ties ancient biblical death practices to modern ones, claiming the dead does the same.

Afterword

Death practices are so long lived that they preserved ancient customs for centuries and narrowed the religious gap dividing Canaanite from Israelite. Biblical death practices still permeate modern Judaism, as even nonobservant Jews tear their clothes as a sign of mourning.

When the long-lived death practices and beliefs of the biblical world finally did change, they did so as reflections of the changing identities of the people. As the Israelites left ancient Israel and became a Diaspora people (the Jews), they needed an afterlife rather than an underworld. Similarly the Jews of the Talmudic period looked for biblical prooftexts to justify their own death traditions, in order to keep their identity as biblically oriented Jews clear and visible.

Most strikingly, in their stability and overall changelessness, death practices have a transformative power. People in both the world of the Bible and in the modern world have used death to transform either themselves or others. By treating him properly, an Israelite could transform an angry ancestor into a protective one. By burying a family member on a piece of land that did not belong to him, an Israelite could transform that land into his own, claiming it for his family. By reburying the skeletal remains of premodern Jews and Israelites in modern Jewish funerals, modern Ultra-Orthodox Jews transform them into something they were not and transform their own role in modern society to that of guardian of the religion.

This transformative power, and how people throughout the ages have used it, is the last word on death. In spite of vast movements over time and space, the death practices of the biblical world have persisted because they remain necessary to living people, and because they still have a role in modern religious and political worlds. Death in the Bible remains the hinge on which many modern death-related issues turn. This, more than anything else, speaks to the persistence of ancient beliefs about death and afterlife, and the ancient burial practices that accompanied them.

Appendix

Chronology 1. Listing of biblical events (all dates approximate):

Undatable	Garden of Eden
Undatable	Story of Noah
c2000 B.C.E.	Abraham
c1700 B.C.E.	The Joseph cycle of stories
c1200 B.C.E.	Moses and the Exodus from Egypt
c1200–1050 B.C.E.	Biblical period of the Judges
c1050–920 B.C.E.	Period of the United Monarchy of Israel (Kings Saul, David, and Solomon)
920–722/586 B.C.E.	Period of the Divided Monarchy of Israel
722 B.C.E.	Fall of Northern Monarchy of Israel
586 B.C.E.	Fall of Southern Kingdom of Judah and beginning of the Babylonian Exile
6th and 5th C B.C.E.	Prophets Isaiah, Jeremiah, and Ezekiel
539–332 B.C.E.	Persian period
332–1st C B.C.E.	Greek period
1st C–5th C C.E.	Roman and Byzantine Christian periods

Chronology 2. Archaeological time periods (all dates approximate):

9000–4500 B.C.E.	Neolithic period
4500–3200 B.C.E.	Chalcolithic period
3200–2200 B.C.E.	Early Bronze Age
2200–2000 B.C.E.	Intermediate Bronze Age
2000–1550 B.C.E.	Middle Bronze Age
1550–1200 B.C.E.	Late Bronze Age
1200–1000 B.C.E.	Iron Age I
1000–6th C B.C.E.	Iron Age II
6th C–4th C B.C.E.	Persian period
4th C–1st C B.C.E.	Greek period
1st C–5th C C.E.	Roman and Byzantine Christian periods

Chronology 3. Listing of key biblical events by book in which they are recorded:

Genesis:
- Garden of Eden
- Story of Noah
- Abraham
- Joseph cycle of stories

Exodus:
- Moses and the Exodus

(Leviticus—largely law codes)
(Numbers—largely law codes)
(Deuteronomy—largely law codes and the death of Moses)

Joshua:
- The conquest of Canaan by Israel

Judges:
The settlement of Canaan
Rule by the Judges

Samuel 1 and 2:
The stories of the United Monarchy, including those of Kings Saul, David, and Solomon

Kings 1 and 2:
The stories of the Divided Monarchy (stories of this period can also be found in 1 and 2 Chronicles)

Isaiah:
The prophecies of Isaiah concerning the destruction of the northern kingdom of Israel and the impending threat to Judah

Jeremiah:
The prophecies of Jeremiah concerning the dismal fate of the exiled Judahites (Jews) in Babylon

Ezekiel:
The prophecies of Ezekiel looking toward ultimate redemption from exile

Notes

Introduction

1. While these documents make the international relationships between Canaan and its neighbors clear, they do not confirm or disprove any specific biblical narratives.

2. Although no writing exists for the early periods, the archaeological and historical chronology of Canaan and Israel traditionally follows that of Egypt. The periods before 3200 B.C.E. are considered prehistoric, while those afterward are considered historic.

3. For the seventh-century date of the writing and/or codification of the Bible, see Israel Finkelstein and Neil Silberman, *The Bible Unearthed: Archaeology's New Vision of Ancient Israel and the Origin of its Sacred Texts* (New York, 2001), 275–285 and Richard Friedman, *Who Wrote the Bible?* (New York, 1987), 136–147.

4. The terms "Canaanite" and "Phoenician" are technically interchangeable, but "Canaanite" is generally applied when discussing the second millennium, while "Phoenician" is used for the first millennium.

5. Philistine settlements are also easily distinguished from both Israelite and Canaanite ones by a certain pottery type and their locations on the southern coastal plain.

6. The southern country was made up of the territory and citizens of only two of the original twelve tribes of Israel, Judah, and Benjamin. Judah had an enormous amount of territory while Ben-

jamin had very little; the new country was named Judah, after the more significant of the two. Judah was always ruled by a descendant of King David.

Most biblical historians agree that the political unity of Israel during the period of the preceding United Monarchy was not as clear as the biblical redactors would like it to have been. The agenda of the Bible referred to above comes deeply into play concerning the literary construction of the United Monarchy. For a good summation of these arguments, see Finkelstein and Silberman, *The Bible Unearthed.*

7. The Samaritans are remembered best through the New Testament story of the "Good Samaritan." The phrase "good Samaritan" epitomizes the differences between Jews and Samaritans. The Judahite legacy of hating the Israelites/Samaritans survived into the first century, making a "good Samaritan" an exception worth noting.

A small group of Samaritans still exists today, living in the vicinity of ancient Samaria. They still uphold ancient traditions such as yearly animal offerings, which Judaism did away with after the destruction of the Second Temple.

Chapter 1: Death in the Biblical World

1. Population estimates are generally made with ethnographic data from modern or nineteenth-century indigenous populations of the Middle East that have settlements similar to ancient ones.

2. See discussions in Elizabeth Bloch-Smith, *Judahite Burial Practices and Beliefs About the Dead* (Sheffield, 1992). Though the percentages are low, this type of burial was common in all the major, well-known cities.

3. There is only one case of an adult buried in a storage jar. The burial is from a northern site called Kfar Yehoshua. The skeleton is actually in two jars, attached end to end.

4. There are exceptions to this rule depending on where the death took place. King Amaziah was killed in Lachish but was brought back to Jerusalem for burial (2 Kings 14.19–20). However, Lachish and Jerusalem are not very far apart.

Josiah, mentioned above, is another partial exception. According to the version of the story recorded in 2 Chronicles, Josiah was wounded in battle near the northern city of Megiddo, but was transported back to Jerusalem by chariot before actually dying. Therefore Josiah was buried with his fathers (2 Chron. 35.24) even though he received his wound in another place.

5. Ossuaries are discussed in more detail in Chapter 3.

6. The next chapter will discuss this care and feeding in detail.

7. One secular possibility is that the fire has to do with the cause of Asa's death. Asa died from an unspecified disease of the feet and is criticized for asking doctors for help rather than asking God for help (2 Chron. 16.12). The fire might have been kindled as a sort of purification either for his sin or for the disease itself.

Chapter 2: The Cult of the Dead in Ancient Israel

1. For a more detailed description of how the Book of Judges may have taken license with the history of the tribes, and how each tribe was most likely governed independently even during times of war, and for how Saul acquired his territory, see Gosta Ahlstrom, *The History of Ancient Palestine* (Minneapolis, 1993), Chapter 8.

2. The Ishmaelites, descendants of Abraham's other son Ishmael, were, according to biblical references, a Bedu tribe at this point. They presumably practiced circumcision during the thirteenth year, as modern Islam does today, following the biblical story of Ishmael's circumcision.

3. Oddly, this story about Saul and the Witch of En Dor has been preserved more than once in American popular culture. The witch of a mother-in-law "Endora" on the television show *Be-*

witched was named for the witch of En Dor, as was "Endor," home of the Ewoks, in *Return of the Jedi.*

4. This hypothesis has been put forward previously by Elizabeth Bloch-Smith, *Judahite Burial Practices,* 124 as well as by P. Kyle McCarter, *I Samuel* (New York, 1980), 55, and Jacob J. Finkelstein, "The Genealogy of the Hammurapi Dynasty," in *Journal of Cuneiform Studies* 20: 113–117.

Chapter 3: A History of Death in the Land of the Bible

1. See Chapter 9 for more on intent.

2. This evidence is not directly related to death and burial per se; it is evidence about the life of the individuals rather than their death that happens to be reflected in their skulls. See Chapter 9 for more on coincidental depositions.

3. See Chapter 9 for more on this problem and on the Jericho cemetery in particular.

4. Another possibility is that they were reusing these tombs in order to associate themselves with their predecessors, as a way of legitimizing land claims.

5. A few equid burials have been found from the same time period in the Aegean as well, from the Argolid.

6. The Egyptians who were buried in Late Bronze Age Canaan have distinctive burial practices of their own, described in the discussion of Philistine burials, below.

7. Greek art contemporary with these ossuaries includes patterns such as running spirals, as well as many better-developed themes. The fifth and fourth centuries B.C.E. are the height of the art of Classical Greece.

8. Acrosolia were not exclusively carved as a place to put ossuaries, in fact, they first became common in the Iron Age. Their subdivisions include "bench tombs," where the individual chambers each contain a bench on which a body would have been

placed. A further subdivision within bench tombs consists of benches with headrests. The head of the deceased was meant to be cradled by these headrests. Many of these headrests are shaped like the wig of the Egyptian goddess Hathor.

Chapter 4: The Death Customs and Beliefs of Israel's Neighbors

1. In both flood stories, a single man is chosen to survive the flood by the gods or by the one God in the Bible. He is told to build an ark according to detailed specifications and then brings every species of animal on board. The flood then destroys the rest of humankind, and when the waters recede the man sends out ravens and doves to search for land. While these details are extraordinarily similar, the biblical version begins by putting forward a religious reason for the flood—mankind was sinful, and therefore needed to be destroyed. In the Mesopotamian version the gods bring the flood because mankind is too noisy. Similarly, the biblical version ends with God's promise never to send another flood again, while the Mesopotamian version makes no such promise for the future, ending with one of the gods becoming angry when he discovers that a single man survived.

2. Utnapishtim is one of the names for the Mesopotamian Noah—he is the one who lived through the flood and who tells the flood story as an aside.

3. See below for a full discussion of She'ol.

4. All quotes from Near Eastern texts cited here can be found in James Pritchard, *Ancient Near Eastern Texts Relating to the Old Testament* (Princeton, N.J., 1969).

5. For a full description of this theme, and its explication in these myths, see Johannes C. deMoor, "Lovable Death in the Ancient Near East" in *Vgarit-Forschungen* 22 (1990): 233–245.

6. Ishtar wants to pay her respects because her brother, who happens to be Ereshkigal's first husband, has died.

7. There are clear parallels to the Greek myth of Persephone. More significantly, this myth was central to Mesopotamian religion. It was acted out during the Babylonian New Year's festival from prehistory through the late first millennium. Evidence comes from representations on a prehistoric (Uruk period) vase, as well as from Neo-Babylonian religious and ritual texts.

8. The variant spellings are different representations of the Hebrew letter "vav," or "wow," a consonant that also serves a vowel-like role.

9. There is no archaeological evidence for sheepskin shrouds, nor should any be expected. Sheepskin is organic, and only in rare or exceptional cases has any organic material survived in the archaeological record of Canaan.

10. The various conflicting lengths of mourning in the Bible will be discussed in more detail in Chapter 7.

Chapter 5: The Biblical Origins of Hell and the Devil

1. For a similar argument see Alan Mintz, "Prayer and the Prayerbook," *Back to the Sources: Reading the Classic Jewish Texts,* Barry W. Holtz, ed. (New York, 1984), 403–429.

2. There is limited evidence for child sacrifice at Carthage, North Africa (see Samuel Wolff, Lawrence Stager, "Child Sacrifice at Carthage—Religious Rite of Population Control?" in *Biblical Archaeology Review* 10, 1(1984): 30–51). Carthage was a Phoenician colony. The Phoenicians were northern Canaanites who shared the culture of their southern neighbors, and who brought that culture from the biblical second millennium into the Greco-Roman first millennium. The Semitic word "Kinnahu," Canaan, has the same meaning as the Greek word "Phoenike." Both terms refer to the red or purple dye that the coastal Canaanites manufactured from shells of the murex mollusk found along their shores. This dye was used for royal robes.

3. Gehenna is contrasted with "Gan Eden," the Garden of Eden, which is the closest rabbinic term for heaven. A more generic and messianic term for the afterlife is "Olam HaBah," the next world.

4. The last, late Shah of Iran carried a staff with an image of Ahura Mazda, the Zoroastrian god, on its top. The name of the automobile manufacturer Mazda is also a modern nod toward Ahura Mazda.

5. Josephus, who in his later years took on the name Flavius in honor of the Roman Flavian dynasty, has an interesting background of his own. He began his career as a general in an army of Jewish rebels who fought against Rome in the Great Revolt of 66 C.E. He was captured but the Roman emperor granted him his life. He lived out his days in Rome, writing histories, including that of the Great Revolt itself, and a history of the Jews.

6. The populace of the secluded desert fortress of Masada, the last stand in the Great Revolt against Rome, may have been Essene. These Jews committed mass suicide rather than be conquered by the Romans.

Chapter 6: Resurrection and Lack of Death in the Bible

1. And in Greek, "Christos." The Romans executed Jesus as a political prisoner, not a religious one, as they thought that he might actually become a king for the Jews and as such was a real threat to Roman rule. The epithet "christ" originally implied that Jesus was to be a human, anointed king (christos, messiah), rather than an eschatological Messiah.

2. This is, of course, a simplification. In both religions there are specific events that will precede the coming of the Messiah. The salient difference between the Messianic beliefs of the two religions is that in Christianity people await the return of the Messiah (Jesus), while in Judaism people await the initial arrival of the Messiah.

Chapter 7: Death in Rabbinic Judaism

1. The bulk of biblical writings were completed by the end of the Persian period, c330 B.C.E., however the Book of Daniel was written later than the rest, in the second century B.C.E.

2. A complicated addendum to this tradition is that the mourning year is often only observed for eleven months.

3. These fears were shared by many later societies. In Victorian England bells were tied to the toes of dead bodies so that if a person woke up in a grave, he would be able to get the attention of the cemetery workers.

4. The very existence of an "Angel of Death" is a development of Rabbinic Judaism that did not originate with the Bible—it most likely derived from Pharisaic beliefs (see Chapter 5).

5. Cremation was never a common option within Jewish communities because by cremating a body, one destroys the body given by God, rather than allowing God to take it back through the process of decomposition. Cremation was occasionally practiced in the biblical world, though cremated burials make up a very small percentage of the whole. Interestingly, cremation still accounts for only approximately 5 percent of disposals in America today.

6. A similar motivation is behind the practice of not burying suicides within a Jewish cemetery (a practice that is generally loopholed within modern Judaism). Only God can bestow life and death, and suicides were therefore thought of as tampering with God's plan. Such tampering was so sinful that its punishment was a posthumous excommunication—the body of such a person should not be with those of decent members of the Jewish community.

Chapter 8: Jewish Death in the Modern World

1. For the purposes of this chapter, we are equating "modern" with "Western." It should be remembered, however, that regions

still exist today where people practice traditional customs and do not have access to (or alternately reject) modern technology.

2. For the purposes of this discussion, death is assumed in old age, rather than the death of a young person from injury or disease.

3. For detailed analyses of both the American funeral industry and the American way of acknowledging and denying death, see Jessica Mitford, *The American Way of Death* (New York, 1963), and Peter Metcalf and Richard Huntington, *Celebrations of Death: The Anthropology of Mortuary Rituals* (Cambridge, England, 1992).

4. Another, more obscure, modern Jewish custom is the placing of pebbles on a grave. This is presumably done to emphasize the differences between Judaism and Christianity, as Christians leave flowers.

5. The numbers quoted here are from a Gallup survey the results of which were partially published in the *New York Times Magazine*, December 7, 1997. The other survey was for *Time*, March 24, 1997.

Chapter 9: A History of Mortuary Theory

1. The work of van Gennep will not be discussed in any detail here, however, his theory of death as a three-staged process—alive, dying, dead—is also applicable to the biblical world.

2. Lewis Binford, "Mortuary Practices: Their Study and Their Potential," in *Approaches to Social Dimensions of Mortuary Practices*, James A. Brown, ed. (1971).

3. Modern examples of this include the way the international community watched the preparations for the funerals of President Kennedy and Princess Diana, as well as the funerals themselves.

4. Since Tainter's initial work, cluster analysis has become an almost standard visual aid to mortuary studies. However, even this relatively simple statistic is not as visually useful as a basic bar or line graph (see below).

5. The two studies are: Talia Shay, "Burial Customs at Jericho in the Intermediate Bronze Age: A Componential Analysis," in *Tel Aviv* 10 (1985): 26–37 and Gaetano Palumbo, " 'Egalitarian' or 'Stratified' Society? Some Notes on Mortuary Practices and Social Structure at Jericho in EB IV," in *Bulletin of the American Schools of Oriental Research* 267 (1987): 43–59. The fact these studies and one additional study turned to the Jericho data is telling. Jericho is one of only two sites in Israel that has enough mortuary data to form a statistically viable database. The other site is Megiddo.

For a partial explanation of why so few sites yield adequate databases, see the discussion of tomb looting in the following chapter.

6. Terminology borrowed from John O'Shea, *Mortuary Variability: An Archaeological Investigation* (New York, 1984), 24.

Chapter 10: The Politics of Death in Israel

1. The same Temple Mount is also the location of Muslim holy sites, such as the Dome of the Rock.

2. Pre-Iron Age burials are less of an issue, as even these groups are beginning to recognize that prehistoric burials cannot be of Israelites.

Bibliography

The following is a partial bibliography of books relating to death and death in the biblical world. Only English sources have been included, and only those that are most relevant to the material discussed in the text.

Gosta Ahlstrom. *The History of Ancient Palestine.* Minneapolis, 1993.

William F. Albright. "The Israelite Conquest of Canaan in Light of Archaeology." *Bulletin of the American Schools of Oriental Research* 74 (1939): 11–23.

Albrecht Alt. *Essays on Old Testament History and Religion.* Oxford, England, 1966.

John Baines and Jaromir Malek. *Atlas of Ancient Egypt.* New York, 1985.

Brad Bartel. "A Historical Review of Ethnological and Archaeological Analyses of Mortuary Practice." *Journal of Anthropological Archaeology* 1 (1982): 32–58.

John R. Bartlett. *Jericho.* Grand Rapids, Mich., 1982.

Amnon Ben-Tor. *The Archaeology of Ancient Israel.* New Haven, Conn., 1992.

Lewis R. Binford. "Archaeology as Anthropology." *American Antiquity* 28 (1962): 217–225.

———. "Mortuary Practices: Their Study and Their Potential." In *Approaches to the Social Dimensions of Mortuary Prac-*

tices, edited by James A. Brown. Part of the series *Memoirs of the Society for American Archaeology* 25 (1971): 6–29.

Elizabeth Bloch-Smith. *Judahite Burial Practices and Beliefs about the Dead.* Sheffield, England, 1992.

Yitzchok Breitowitz. "The Desecration of Graves in Eretz Yisrael: The Struggle to Honor the Dead and Preserve Our Historical Legacy." www.jlaw.com/Articles/heritage.html. Feb. 28, 2001.

Jan M. Bremer, Theo P. J. van den Hout, and Rudolph Peters, eds. *Hidden Futures: Death and Immortality in Ancient Egypt, Anatolia, the Classical, Biblical and Arabic-Islamic World.* Amsterdam, 1994.

Herbert C. Brichto. "Kin, Cult, Land and Afterlife—A Biblical Complex." *Hebrew Union College Annual* 44 (1973): 1–54.

Robert Chapman, Ian Kinnes, and Klaus Randsborg, eds. *The Archaeology of Death.* Cambridge, England, 1981.

Abraham Cohen and Jacob Neusner. *Everyman's Talmud: The Major Teachings of the Rabbinic Sages.* New York, 1995.

Shaye Cohen. *The Beginnings of Jewishness.* Berkeley, Calif., 1999.

Richard Craze. *Hell: An Illustrated History.* Berkeley, Calif., 1996.

John Currid. *Ancient Egypt and the Old Testament.* Grand Rapids, Mich., 1997.

Johannes C. de Moor. "Lovable Death in the Ancient Near East." *Ugarit-Forschungen* 22 (1990): 233–245.

William G. Dever. "Funerary Practices in EBIV (MBI) Palestine: A Study in Cultural Discontinuity." in *Love and Death in the Ancient Near East: Essays in Honor of Marvin Pope,* edited by John H. Marks and Robert M. Good, 9–19. Guilford, Conn., 1987.

Anita Diamant. *Saying Kaddish.* New York, 1998.

Trude Dothan. *The Philistines and Their Material Culture.* Jerusalem, 1982.

Amos Elon. "Politics and Archaeology." In *The Archaeology*

of Israel, Constructing the Past, Interpreting the Future, edited by Neil A. Silberman and David Small, 34–47. Sheffield, England, 1997.

Israel Finkelstein and Neil A. Silberman. *The Bible Unearthed: Archaeology's New Vision of Ancient Israel and the Origin of its Sacred Texts.* New York, 2001.

Richard Friedman. *Who Wrote the Bible?* New York, 1987.

Neil Gilman. *The Death of Death: Resurrection and Immortality in Jewish Thought.* Woodstock, Vt., 1997.

Norman Gottwald. *The Tribes of Yahweh.* New York, 1979.

Rachel Hallote. "Mortuary Archaeology and the Middle Bronze Age Southern Levant." *Journal of Mediterranean Archaeology* 8, 1 (1995): 93–125.

Baruch Halpern. "The Excremental Vision: The Doomed Priests of Doom in Isaiah 28." *Hebrew Annual Review* 10 (1986): 109–121.

Robert Hertz. "A Contribution to the Study of the Collective Representation of Death." In *Death and the Right Hand,* translated by Rodney Needham and Claudia Needham. New York, 1960 (originally 1907).

Ian Hodder. "Burials, Houses, Women and Men in the European Neolithic." In *Ideology, Power and Prehistory,* edited by Daniel Miller and Chris Tilley, 51–68. Cambridge, England, 1984.

Barry Holtz, ed. *Back to the Sources: Reading the Classic Jewish Texts.* New York, 1984.

Kathleen Howard. *Treasures of the Holy Land: Ancient Art from the Israel Museum.* New York, 1986.

David Ilan. "Mortuary Practices at Tel Dan in the Middle Bronze Age: A Reflection of Canaanite Society and Ideology." In *The Archaeology of Death in the Ancient Near East,* edited by Stuart Campbell and Anthony Green, 117–139. Oxford, England, 1995.

Martin Jaffee. *Early Judaism.* Upper Saddle River, N.J., 1997.

Kathleen Kenyon. *Excavations at Jericho. Volume One: The Tombs Excavated in 1952–4.* London, 1960.

———. *Excavations at Jericho. Volume Two: The Tombs Excavated in 1955–8.* London, 1965.

Maurice Lamm. *The Jewish Way in Death and Mourning.* New York, 1969.

Bernhard Lang. "Life after Death in the Prophetic Promise." In *Supplement to Vetus Testumentum 40,* edited by J. A. Emerton, 144–156. Leiden, Netherlands, 1988.

Thomas Levy, ed. *The Archaeology of Society in the Holy Land.* London, 1993.

John H. Marks and Robert M. Good, eds. *Love and Death in the Ancient Near East: Essays in Honor of Marvin Pope.* Guilford, Conn., 1987.

Simon Mays. *The Archaeology of Human Bones.* London, 1998.

Amichai Mazar. *Archaeology of the Land of the Bible, 10,000–586 B.C.E.* New York, 1990.

George Mendenhall. "The Hebrew Conquest of Palestine." *Biblical Archaeologist* 25 (1962): 66–87.

Peter Metcalf and Richard Huntington. *Celebrations of Death: The Anthropology of Mortuary Rituals.* Cambridge, England, 1992.

Jessica Mitford. *The American Way of Death.* New York, 1963.

Ian Morris. *Death-Ritual and Social Structure in Classical Antiquity.* Cambridge, England, 1992.

Jacob Neusner. *The Talmud.* Lanham, Md., 1995.

John O'Shea. *Mortuary Variability: An Archaeological Investigation.* New York, 1984.

James B. Pritchard, ed. *Ancient Near Eastern Texts Relating to the Old Testament.* Princeton, N.J., 1969.

Simcha P. Raphael. *Jewish Views of the Afterlife.* Northvale, N.J., 1994.

Jack Reimer. *Jewish Insights on Death and Mourning.* New York, 1995.

Brian Schmidt. *Israel's Beneficent Dead: Ancestor Cult and Necromancy in Ancient Israelite Religion and Tradition.* Winona Lake, Ind., 1996.

Michael Shanks and Chris Tilley. *Social Theory and Archaeology.* Albuquerque, N.Mex., 1987.

———. *Reconstructing Archaeology.* New York, 1992.

Yaacov Shavit. "Archaeology, Political Culture, and Culture in Israel." In *The Archaeology of Israel, Constructing the Past, Interpreting the Future,* edited by Neil A. Silberman and David Small, 48–61. Sheffield, England, 1997.

Morton Smith. *Palestine Parties and Politics that Shaped the Old Testament.* New York, 1971.

John A. Tainter. "Social Inference and Mortuary Practices: An Experiment in Numerical Classification." *World Archaeology* 7 (1975): 1–15.

Alice Turner. *A History of Hell.* New York, 1993.

Peter J. Ucko. "Ethnography and Archaeological Interpretation of Funerary Remains." *World Archaeology* 1 (1969): 261–280.

Arnold van Gennep. *The Rites of Passage.* Translated by Monika Vizedom and Gabrielle Caffee. Chicago, 1960 (originally 1908).

Nico van Uchelen. "Death and the Afterlife in the Hebrew Bible of Ancient Israel." In *Hidden Futures: Death and Immortality in Ancient Egypt, Anatolia, the Classical, Biblical and Arabic-Islamic World,* edited by Jan M. Bremer, Theo P. J. van den Hout, and Rudolph Peters, 79–90. Amsterdam, 1994.

Geoffrey Wigoder. *The Encyclopedia of Judaism.* Jerusalem, 1989.

Index

Aaron, death of, 43, 163
Abraham, 103, 125, 210, 211, 215n. 2; arrival in Canaan, 14–15, 18; buries wife in Canaanite tomb, 15, 39; death of, 42, 43, 118; as monotheist, 14–15
Absalom, 50
Acrosolia tombs, 39–40, 99, 135, 188, 216n. 8
Adam and Eve, 14, 15, 105–106, 161
Adapa, myth of, 106–107
Afterlife, the: biblical She'ol, 43, 53, 107–110, 111–114, 122, 125, 126, 127–128, 134, 208; Egyptian attitudes toward, 115, 117; heaven, 122, 127–128, 130–131, 149, 178–179, 219n. 3; hell, 122, 125, 126–128, 129, 134, 178–179, 219n. 3; Israelite attitudes toward, 43, 52–53, 107–110, 112–114, 121–122, 208, 209; Jewish attitudes toward, 122, 126, 127–128, 129–131, 135, 148–149, 152, 167–168, 208, 219n. 3; Mesopotamian Netherworld, 107–110; and near-death experiences, 177–178; in Rabbinic Judaism, 126, 130, 148–149, 152, 167–168, 219n. 3; and tomb offerings, 71, 111–114, 141. *See also* Cult of the Dead.
Ahlstrom, Gosta, 215n. 1
Albright, William Foxwell, 18
Alt, Albrecht, 19
Amarna archive, 14, 90
Amaziah, 215n. 4
Ancestor worship, 51, 61–62, 66–67, 71, 73, 74–75, 102, 181. *See also* Cult of the Dead.
Aninut, 164, 165
Asa, 51–52, 215n. 7
Asherah, 54, 58
Assyria, 21–22, 63, 93

Ba'al, 54, 58, 112
Bab edh-Dhra, 78–80
Babylon, 85, 133–134; Judah destroyed by, 22, 93, 95, 123, 134, 147, 166, 210, 212; Judahites exiled to, 22, 123–125, 126, 147, 152, 166, 168, 169, 212
Bead tombs, 80, 82
Bedouin burials, 199, 200–202
Beelzebub, 133
Beer Sheba, 41
Bench tombs, 216n. 6
Bible, Hebrew: burial markers mentioned in, 47–51; *Epic of Gilgamesh* compared to, 104, 105–107, 217nn. 1, 2; and Judahites, 22–23; lack of death in, 144–147; Mesopotamia in, 14–15, 103–104; mourning practices in, 146, 153–154, 162–163; necromancy in the, 58–60; references to "breath of life" in, 75–77, 78; references to death in, 12, 15, 28–29, 42–45, 47–53, 70, 113–114, 187, 218n. 8; relationship

Bible, Hebrew (*cont.*)
to Talmud, 151–152; reliability of, 12, 14–15, 18–20; resurrection in, 137–142, 143, 155. *See also* Abraham; Adam and Eve; Canaanites; Flood, the; Garden of Eden; Israelites; Judahites; New Testament; Philistines; Satan; *specific books.*
Binford, Lewis, 185–188
Borneo, 181–182
Bronze Age: Cult of the Dead during, 54; Early Bronze Age, 70, 78–80; houses during, 36–37; infant burials during, 37; Intermediate Bronze Age, 80–84, 190, 211; Iron Age compared to, 33, 36–37, 39–40, 71, 99, 100; Late Bronze Age, 88–90, 93, 192, 211; Middle Bronze Age, 33, 37, 69–70, 71, 84–88, 190, 192, 211; tombs during, 33, 37–38, 39
Burial Kaddish, 155, 163
Burial location, 44–45, 79, 116, 117, 118, 121, 215n. 4; in cemeteries, 30, 37–38, 39, 41–42, 45–46, 64, 78–80, 86, 188, 190, 205; in fields, 30, 33–35, 176, 206–207, 208, 216n. 4; under houses, 30, 36–39, 46, 64, 86, 88, 103, 187–188. *See also* Tombs.
Burial markers, 45–51, 78
Burial practices: burial within a day of death, 174, 198; during Chalcolithic period, 75–78, 98, 100, 182; changes in, 69, 75, 123, 169, 170, 208; continuity in, 11, 69–70, 81–82, 85, 90, 95, 97, 100, 102, 134–135, 169–170, 206–207, 208–209; during Early Bronze Age, 78–80, 81–82; intent exhibited by, 190–193; during Intermediate Bronze Age, 80–84, 190; during Iron Age, 33, 35, 37–38, 39–40, 46, 70–72, 91, 93–95, 96, 199; during Late Bronze Age, 88–90, 192, 216n. 6; during Middle Bronze Age, 33, 37, 69–72, 84–88, 85, 190, 192, 216n. 4; in modern world, 172–175; during Neolithic period, 72–75, 182; during Persian/Hellenistic periods, 95–100; secondary burials, 76, 79–80, 82, 99–100, 181–182, 188, 196–197; and social structure, 31–33, 186–188, 192, 221n. 3; statistical analyses of, 188–190, 193, 221n. 4, 222n. 5; during Talmudic period, 32–33, 34, 196, 197; tomb offerings, 70–72, 82, 87–88, 141, 161–162, 192, 216n. 5; transformative power of, 208–209. *See also* Burial location; Mourning practices; Tombs.

Canaanites: assimilation of, 17–18, 85, 93; burial practices of, 19, 20, 38, 64, 80, 84–88, 115–117, 182, 184, 192, 199, 206, 216n. 4, 218n. 9; child sacrifice among, 125–126; Cult of the Dead among, 53, 54, 58, 64, 68, 91, 102, 111–112, 113; Egyptians compared to, 116–117; god of death among, 112–114; Israelites compared to, 14, 17–18, 20, 22, 38, 53, 57–58, 64–65, 68, 91, 111–112, 113, 184, 208, 213n. 5; Judahites compared to, 23, 64–65; Mesopotamians compared to, 112; Phoenicians as, 17, 218n. 2; relations with Egyptians, 81, 85, 87, 88–89, 90, 94–95; relations with Greeks, 89–90; relations with Israelites, 15–20, 57–58, 84, 90, 91, 93, 113, 125–126; relations with Philistines, 84, 90; writing among, 14, 182
Carthage, 218n. 2
Cemeteries, 30, 37–38, 39, 41–42, 45–46, 64, 78–80, 86, 188, 205;

Jericho cemetery, 72–73, 74, 80, 82–83, 182, 190, 222n. 5
Chalcolithic period, 70, 75–78, 98, 100, 182, 211
Chanukah, 128
Child burials, 37–38, 166–167
Child sacrifice, 125–126, 218n. 2
Christianity: Jesus, 96, 142–143; Judaism compared to, 97–98, 122, 125, 130, 133, 134, 143–144, 147–148, 156, 161, 170, 177–179, 219n. 2, 221n. 4; messianic philosophy in, 147–148, 219nn. 1, 2; resurrection in, 142–144. *See also* New Testament.
1 Chronicles, 212
2 Chronicles, 212; 16.12, 215n. 7; 16.14, 51–52; 26.23, 44; 29.27, 44; 35.24, 215n. 4
Circumcision, 57, 167, 215n. 2
Cleansing of bodies, 159–161, 198
Coffins, 46, 89, 93–95, 96–98, 120, 121, 161, 172–173
Cremation, 48–49, 78–79, 220n. 5
Cult of the Dead: attitude of Judahites toward, 22–23, 63; among Canaanites, 53, 54, 58, 64, 68, 91, 102, 111–112, 113; and immortality, 12; among Israelites, 11–12, 53, 54–68, 91, 101, 111–112, 113, 208; necromancy in, 58–61, 67; and Saul, 55–61; as threat to monotheism, 53, 54–55, 63, 64–65, 67–68; as threat to United Monarchy, 53, 61–62. *See also* Afterlife, the.

Dagger tombs, 80, 82
Dan, 21
Daniel, book of, 220n. 1; 10.2, 163–164; 12.2, 148
David, 61, 92, 210, 212, 214n. 6; death of, 44; Jerusalem captured by, 20; relationship with Saul, 55–56, 58, 68
Dead, the: attitudes of Israelites toward, 11–12, 28–30, 33–35, 48–49, 51, 60–61, 65–68, 176, 197–198, 208; attitudes of Jews toward, 196–198, 220nn. 5, 6; attitudes of Judahites toward, 29–30, 33–35; communication with, 58–61; euphemisms for, 28–29, 42–45, 172; fear of, 12, 29, 61, 68, 176; and God, 52–53, 109–110; sacrifices for, 66–67; social role of, 29–30, 33–35. *See also* Ancestor worship; Cult of the Dead; Death.
Death: attitudes of Israelites toward, 11, 12, 15, 52–53, 65–66, 100–101, 103–104, 107–110, 112–114, 121–122, 209; attitudes of Jews toward, 11, 123–124, 130, 152, 154–158, 169–171, 172–176, 179, 220n. 6; attitudes of Mesopotamians toward, 66–67, 104–111, 114; attitudes of modern Jews toward, 11, 169–171, 172–176, 179, 220n. 6; attitudes of Rabbinic Judaism toward, 130, 152, 154–158, 220nn. 4, 6; biblical references to, 12, 15, 28–29, 42–45, 47–53, 70, 113–114, 187, 218n. 8; by suicide, 220n. 6; denial of, 171–173, 174–175, 221n. 3; fear of, 11, 52–53, 68, 104, 107, 110, 175–176; and God, 157, 158, 176, 220nn. 5, 6; gods and goddesses of, 110–114; inevitability of, 104, 157–158, 171, 175–176; and technology, 170–171, 175–176, 177, 179; theories of, 180–184. *See also* Dead, the.
Deuteronomy, 211; 15.1–3, 34; 15.9–10, 34; 18.10–11, 58; 21.13, 164; 26.13–14, 65; 34.8, 163
Devil, the, 125, 131–134
Dolmens, 83–84
Donkey burials, 87–88

Early Bronze Age. *See* Bronze Age.
Ecclesiastes, book of; 5.15, 159
Egypt: burial practices in, 38, 41, 94, 96, 101, 114–115, 116, 117, 118–120, 121, 216n. 6; coffins in, 94, 96; embalming in, 115, 118–120; Hyksos in, 87, 88; relations with Canaan, 81, 85, 87, 88–89, 90, 94–95; relations with Israel, 13; relations with Philistines, 92–93, 94–95; tombs in, 38, 41, 115, 116; writing in, 13–14
Elijah, 143, 145–147
Elisha, 139–141, 143, 145–147
Embalming, 115, 118–120, 172, 173
Enoch, 15, 144–145
Epic of Gilgamesh, 104–107, 217nn. 1, 2
Equid burials, 87–88, 216n. 5
Ereshkigal, 110–111, 112, 217n. 6, 218n. 7
Essenes, 128, 219n. 6
Evil, 124–125
Exodus, book of, 211; 14.18, 120; 22.18, 58; 23.10–11, 34
Exodus, the, 18, 19–20, 120, 210, 211
Ezekiel, book of, 147, 210, 212; 36.25, 159, 160; 37.3–11, 137–138

Fear: of the dead, 12, 29, 61, 68, 176; of death, 11, 52–53, 68, 104, 107, 110, 175–176; of false death, 157, 220n. 3
Fields, burial in, 30, 33–35, 176, 206–207, 208, 216n. 4
Flood, the, 104, 217nn. 1, 2
Frazer, James, 181
Functionalism, 183

Gamliel II, Rabbi, 97–98, 161
Garden of Eden, 103, 210, 211, 219n. 3
Genesis, book of, 211; 2.7, 75; 2.10–14, 103; 3.19, 97, 105; 5.21–24, 144; 12.6, 15; 12.8, 15; 14.18–19, 15, 120; 25.8, 42; 25.9–11, 42; 35.8, 48; 35.19–20, 50; 37.35, 109; 37.5, 109; 49.29–32, 118; 50.2–3, 119; 50.4–14, 119; 50.10, 163; 50.22–26, 120
Gennep, Arnold van, 181, 221n. 1
God: and cremation, 220n. 5; and the dead, 52–53, 109–110; and death, 157, 158, 176, 220nn. 5, 6; and evil, 124–125; relationship with Satan, 131–133; and resurrection, 137–139; and suicide, 220n. 6; as Yahweh, 19, 20–21, 22, 57–58, 64, 67–68, 125
Golan Heights, 77, 83–84
Gottwald, Norman, 19
Greeks: burial practices of, 89–90; relations with Canaanites, 89–90; relations with Jews, 127, 128–129, 134, 210, 211

Heaven, 127–128, 178–179, 219n. 3; Jewish attitudes toward, 122, 127, 129, 130–131, 149. *See also* Afterlife, the.
Hell: American attitudes toward, 178–179; as Gehenna, 126, 219n. 3; Jewish attitudes toward, 125, 129, 130–131; She'ol compared to, 122, 125, 126, 127–128, 134; and Zoroastrianism, 126–128, 129. *See also* Afterlife, the.
Hertz, Robert, 181–182
Hevra Kaddisha, 160, 162–163
Hodder, Ian, 38
Hospice movement, 177
Houses: during Bronze Age, 36–37; during Iron Age, 17, 36–37, 40; ossuaries compared to, 77–78, 98–99; tombs under, 30, 36–39, 46, 64, 86, 88, 103, 187–188
Huntington, Richard, 221n. 3
Hyksos, 87, 88

Hypotheses, 185

Immortality, 12, 104, 105–107, 114, 148
Infant burials, 37–38
Iron Age, 211; Bronze Age compared to, 33, 36–37, 39–40, 71, 99, 100; coffins during, 96; houses during, 17, 36–37, 40; tombs during, 33, 35, 37–38, 39–40, 46. *See also* Canaanites; Israelites; Philistines.
Isaiah, book of, 28–29, 210, 212; 14.3–4, 134; 14.12–15, 134; 14.15, 109; 26.19, 108; 28.15, 114; 28.17–19, 114; 38.18, 109; 45.7, 124; 65.2–6, 63
Ishmael, 215n. 2
Ishtar, 111, 112, 217n. 6, 218n. 7
Islam, 215n. 2, 222n. 1
Israel, ancient: relations with Egypt, 13; relations with Mesopotamia, 13; role of family in, 46, 53, 91, 206; social role of the dead in, 29–30, 33–35; social structure in, 31, 32–33, 61–62; writing in, 13–14. *See also* Canaanites; Israelites; Judahites; Philistines.
Israel, kingdom of: destruction of, 21–22, 28, 62–63, 93, 210, 212; relations with Judah, 20–21, 62
Israel, modern State of: antiquities trade in, 203–204; Ministry of Religious Affairs in, 194–195, 198–199; tree planting in, 49; Ultra-Orthodox Jews in, 195, 196–199, 202, 205–207, 208–209
Israelites: attitudes toward the afterlife, 43, 52–53, 107–110, 112–114, 121–122, 208, 209; attitudes toward the dead, 11–12, 28–30, 33–35, 48–49, 51, 60–61, 65–68, 176, 197–198, 208; attitudes toward death, 11, 12, 15, 52–53, 65–66, 100–101, 103–104, 107–110, 112–114, 121–122, 209; attitudes toward resurrection, 137–142, 143–144, 149; burial practices of, 19, 20, 29–53, 64, 70–72, 86, 91, 99, 103, 115–121, 137, 141–142, 160, 161–162, 176, 184, 187–189, 197–198, 199, 206, 208–209, 216n. 8, 218n. 9; Canaanites compared to, 14, 17–18, 20, 22, 38, 53, 57–58, 64–65, 68, 91, 111–112, 113, 184, 208, 213n. 5; Cult of the Dead among, 11–12, 53, 54–68, 91, 101, 102, 111–112, 113, 208; defined, 22; dietary laws among, 57; Egyptians compared to, 116, 117, 212; Judahites compared to, 20–23; Mesopotamians compared to, 66–67, 102–103, 107–110, 114; monotheism among, 53, 54, 57–58, 63, 64–65, 67–68, 102, 110, 114; Philistines compared to, 213n. 5; polytheism among, 54–55, 58, 64, 67–68, 112–114, 124; relations with Canaanites, 15–20, 57–58, 84, 90, 91, 93, 113, 125–126; relations with Egyptians, 18, 19–20; relations with Judahites, 20–21, 22–23, 62, 214n. 7; relations with Philistines, 48–49, 56, 57, 58, 59, 91–93, 133; Syrians compared to, 102–103; tithes among, 65–66; writing among, 13–14; Yahweh worshipped by, 19, 20–21, 57–58, 64, 67–68. *See also* Bible, Hebrew; Jews; Judaism, modern; Judaism, Rabbinic.

Jacob, 153; death of, 117–120, 163
Jeremiah, book of, 210, 212; 22.10, 165–166
Jericho, 72–73, 74, 80, 82–83, 182, 190, 222n. 5
Jerusalem, 20–21, 91, 96, 195–196
Jesus: death of, 96, 219n. 1; Lazarus

Jesus (*cont.*)
resurrected by, 142–143;
resurrection of, 143
Jews: attitudes toward afterlife, 122, 126, 127–128, 129–131, 135, 148–149, 152, 167–168, 208, 219n. 3; attitudes toward the dead, 196–198, 220nn. 5, 6; attitudes toward death, 11, 123–124, 130, 152, 154–158, 169–171, 172–176, 179, 220nn. 4, 6; attitudes toward the devil, 125, 131–134; attitudes toward heaven, 122, 127, 129, 130–131, 149; attitudes toward hell, 125, 129, 130–131; attitudes toward Messiah, 147–148, 149, 197, 219n. 2; attitudes toward resurrection, 135, 136–142, 147–149, 152, 155, 163, 167–168, 197; burial practices of, 11, 32–33, 46, 123, 134–135, 169–170, 172–175, 196–198; Christians compared to, 97–98, 122, 125, 130, 133, 134, 143–144, 147–148, 156, 161, 170, 177–179, 219n. 2, 221n. 4; coffins used by, 96–98; defined, 22; Diaspora of, 123–128, 131, 135, 136, 151, 167–168, 208; monotheism among, 124; relations with Christians, 97–98; relations with Greeks, 127, 128–129, 134, 210, 211; relations with Persians, 126–128, 131, 210, 211; relations with Romans, 127, 128, 130, 134, 210, 211; relations with Samaritans, 21; Zoroastrian influence among, 127–128, 129
Job, book of, 165; 1.6–8, 132; 2.12, 132; 17.16, 108, 109
John, gospel of: 11.38–44, 142–143; 19.40, 96; 20, 143
Joseph, 117–119, 153, 163, 210, 211; death of, 120–121
Josephus, 128, 129, 130, 151–152, 219n. 5
Joshua, book of, 16, 18–19, 211; 7.26, 47; 8.29, 47; 10.27, 47; 11.27, 47, 141; 18.6, 126; 24.32, 121
Josiah, 44, 215n. 4
Judah, kingdom of, 212, 213n. 6; Cult of the Dead as threat to, 63; destroyed by Babylonians, 22, 93, 95, 123, 134, 147, 166, 210, 212; relations with Israel, 20–21, 62; Uzziah, 50–51
Judahites: attitudes toward Cult of the Dead, 22–23, 63; attitudes toward the dead, 28–30, 33–35; attitudes toward Israelites, 22; and Bible, 22–23; Canaanites compared to, 23, 64–65; defined, 22; dietary laws among, 63; exiled to Babylon, 22, 123–125, 126, 147, 152, 166, 168, 169, 212; Israelites compared to, 20–23; relations with Israelites, 20–21, 22, 62, 214n. 7; Yahweh worshipped by, 20–21, 22, 63, 64. *See also* Bible, Hebrew; Israelites; Jews.
Judaism, modern: ancient Judaism compared to, 174, 175–176, 179; attitudes toward death in, 11, 169–171, 172–176, 179, 220n. 6; attitudes toward the Messiah in, 197, 219n. 2; attitudes toward resurrection in, 197; burial practices in, 11, 32–33, 169–170, 172–175, 220n. 6; Conservative Jews, 150–151; mourning practices in, 29, 67, 153, 174, 175, 208, 221n. 4; Orthodox Jews, 150–151, 197; Rabbinic Judaism compared to, 67, 169–170, 179, 220n. 6; secularism in, 11, 168, 179; and Talmud, 150–151; Ultra-Orthodox Jews, 195, 196–199, 202, 205–207, 208–209. *See also* Israelites; Jews; Judahites; Judaism, Rabbinic.
Judaism, Rabbinic, 27–28, 100, 129,

144–145; Angel of Death in, 157–158, 220n. 4; attitudes toward afterlife in, 126, 130, 148–149, 152, 167–168, 219n. 3; attitudes toward Bible in, 151, 153–154, 159–160, 164, 165–166, 169, 208; attitudes toward death in, 130, 152, 154–158, 220nn. 4, 6; attitudes toward resurrection in, 137, 147–149, 152, 155, 163, 167–168; biblical Judaism compared to, 123, 151–152, 160, 161–163, 169; burial practices in, 32–33, 35, 159–163, 166–167, 182, 196, 197, 198, 220n. 6; Garden of Eden in, 219n. 3; Gehenna in, 126, 219n. 3; modern Judaism compared to, 67, 169–170, 179, 220n. 6; mourning practices in, 152–155, 162–167, 220n. 2; and Oral Law, 95, 129, 130–131; prooftexts used in, 159–160, 164, 165–166, 169, 208. *See also* Israelites; Jews; Judahites; Judaism, modern; Talmud.
Judges, book of, 16, 18–19, 212, 215n. 1; 2.10, 43; 16, 92

Kennewick Man, 200
Kenyon, Kathleen, 72–73, 82, 190
1 Kings, 212; 2.10, 44; 4, 62; 10.26, 62; 17.28, 44
2 Kings, 212; 2.1, 145, 146; 2.11–12, 146; 4.32–35, 139; 13.20–21, 140; 14.19–20, 215n. 4; 20.22, 44; 23.10, 125; 23.17–18, 50

Lamentations, book of, 165
Lamm, Maurice, 197
Late Bronze Age. *See* Bronze Age.
Lazarus, resurrection of, 142–143
Levi, 161
Lévi-Strauss, Claude, 184
Leviticus, book of, 211; 19.28, 153; 20.6, 59; 20.27, 59; 21.1–7, 34; 25.1–7, 34
Living wills, 171
Lucifer, 133–134
Luke, gospel of: 7.11–17, 96; 14, 143; 23.5–6, 96; 24.51, 143

Maimonides, 148
Malinowski, B., 183
Mark, gospel of: 7.1, 129; 16.1, 96; 16.19, 143; 18, 143
Masada, 195, 219n. 6
Matthew, gospel of: 12.24, 133; 28, 143
Megiddo, 222n. 5
Mendenhall, George, 19
Mesopotamia: ancestor worship in, 66–67; attitudes toward death in, 66–67, 102–103, 104–111, 114; burial practices in, 101, 102–103; goddesses of death in, 110–111, 112; the Netherworld in, 107–110, 121; relations with Israel, 13; writing in, 13–14
Messiah, the, 147–148, 149, 167, 197, 219nn. 1, 2
Metcalf, Peter, 221n. 3
Middle Bronze Age. *See* Bronze Age.
Mintz, Alan, 218n. 1
Mishnah, 35, 151, 162
Mitford, Jessica, 221n. 3
Moloch, 125–126
Moses, 16, 120, 210, 211; death of, 163
Motu, 112, 113–114, 124, 218n. 8
Mourning practices, 183; in Bible, 146, 153–154, 162–163; Burial Kaddish, 155, 163; in modern Judaism, 29, 67, 153, 174, 175, 208, 221n. 4; Mourners' Kaddish, 154–155, 162, 163, 174; in Rabbinic Judaism, 152–155, 162–167, 220n. 2; tearing of clothes, 146, 153, 175, 208. *See also* Burial practices.

Native Americans, 200

Natufian period, 74
Near-death experiences, 177–178
Necromancy, 58–61, 67
Neolithic period, 72–75, 182, 211
New Archaeology, 184–189
New Testament, 96, 129, 133, 141, 151–152; resurrection in, 142–144. *See also* Bible, Hebrew; Christianity.
Noah, 14, 15, 210, 211
Numbers, book of, 211; 13.27–28, 16; 20.26, 43; 20.29, 163; 22.22, 131

Oral Law, 35, 95, 129, 130–131
Ossuaries, 43, 46, 76–78, 98–101, 182, 197, 216nn. 7, 8
Outsized tombs, 80, 82

Paleolithic period, 74
Passover, 145
Persians, 126–128, 131, 210, 211
Pharisees, 128, 129, 130–131, 220n. 4
Philistines: burial practices of, 93–95, 96, 199; Israelites compared to, 213n. 5; relations with Canaanites, 84, 90; relations with Egyptians, 92–93, 94–95; relations with Israelites, 48–49, 56, 57, 58, 59, 91–93, 133
Phoenicians, 17, 218n. 2. *See also* Canaanites.
Pillars, as burial markers, 50
Post-Processual Archaeology, 189–190
Pottery tombs, 82
Processions, funeral, 116, 162–163, 174
Psalms: 6.5, 109; 18.5–6, 109; 22.12–22, 52; 23, 163; 88.4–5, 53, 109; 91, 162–163; 106.28, 67
Purim, 126

Resurrection, 136–144; in Christianity, 142–144; and God, 137–139; Israelite attitudes toward, 137–142, 143–144, 149; Jewish attitudes toward, 135, 136–142, 147–149, 152, 155, 163, 167–168, 197
Romans, 127, 128, 130, 134, 210, 211

Sabbath, 151, 156, 165
Sadducees, 128, 129–130
Samaria, 20–21, 41, 214n. 7
1 Samuel, 212; 1.21, 66; 2.19, 66; 4–6, 92; 8.5, 57; 17, 92; 20.29, 66; 20.6, 66; 28.6–25, 60; 28.8–9, 59; 28.15, 60; 29.4, 131; 31.11–13, 48
2 Samuel, 212; 18.17, 47; 18.18, 50; 22.5–6, 109
Satan, 131–133
Saul, 210, 212; and Cult of the Dead, 55–61; death of, 48–49, 92; necromancy resorted to by, 58–60, 67, 215n. 3; relationship with David, 55–56, 58, 68
Secondary burials, 76, 79–80, 82, 99–100, 181–182, 188, 196–197
Sheloshim, 165
She'ol, 53, 107–110, 111–114, 208; hell compared to, 122, 125, 126, 127–128, 134. *See also* Afterlife, the.
Shiva, 164–165
Shrouds, sheepskin, 116–117, 218n. 9
Shuwala, 113–114, 124
Sinuhe, story of, 115–117, 121
Six Day War, 195, 198
Skull plastering, 72–75, 182
Solomon, 20, 56, 61, 62, 93, 210, 212
Statistical analyses, 188–190, 193, 221n. 4, 222n. 5
Structuralism, 183–184
Syria, 84, 102–103, 113
Systems theory, 185

Tainter, J., 189, 221n. 4
Talmud: Angel of Death in, 157–158, 220n. 4; cleansing of bodies in, 159–161, 198; death in, 154–158;

Mishnah, 35, 151, 162; and modern Judaisim, 150–151; mourning practices mentioned in, 152–155, 162–167; and Oral Law, 35, 95, 129, 130–131; origin of, 95, 129–130, 150–151; and ossuaries, 182; relationship to Bible, 151–152; secondary burial in, 196–197. *See also* Judaism, Rabbinic.
Tearing of clothes, 146, 153, 175, 208
Technology, 170–171, 175–176, 177, 179
Temple, the: First Temple, 20, 51, 129, 195–196; Second Temple, 126, 130, 195–196; Temple Mount, 195–196, 222n. 1
Tithes, 65–66
Tombs: acrosolia, 39–40, 99, 135, 188, 216n. 8; bead tombs, 80, 82; bench tombs, 216n. 8; during Bronze Age, 33, 35, 37–38, 39, 78–88; dagger tombs, 80, 82; in Egypt, 38, 41, 115, 116; as houses for the dead, 38–39, 40–41, 77–78, 98–99, 184; intent exhibited by, 190–193; during Iron Age, 33, 37–38, 39–40, 46; looting of, 203–206; markers for, 45–51; offerings in, 70–72, 82, 87–88, 141, 161–162, 192, 216n. 5; outsized tombs, 80, 82; pottery tombs, 82; sealing of, 141–142, 143, 197; shaft-and-chamber tombs, 35, 39–43, 80, 81–82, 85–86, 91, 99, 135, 188, 216n. 8; and social structure, 31–33, 186–188, 192. *See also* Burial location; Ossuaries.
Trees as burial markers, 48–49
Tylor, E. B., 181

Ugarit, 16, 111–112
Utnapishtim, 105, 217n. 2
Uzziah, 50–51

Witch of En Dor, 59–60, 215n. 3

Yahweh. *See* God.
Yohanan ben Zakkai, Rabbi, 96

Zechariah, book of, 3.1, 131
Zoroastrianism: and the devil, 131; and hell, 126–128, 129; in modern world, 219n. 4

A NOTE ON THE AUTHOR

Rachel S. Hallote was born in New Rochelle, New York, and studied at Bryn Mawr College and the University of Chicago, where she received a Ph.D. in Near Eastern archaeology. She has since done considerable work on the archaeology of death, including excavations in Israel. Ms. Hallote now directs the Jewish Studies Program at Purchase College of the State University of New York, and teaches in the program. She lives in New Rochelle.